Rust Programming for Web Assembly

Build Blazing-Fast, Next-Gen Web Applications

Jeff Stuart

Discover Other Books in the Series

"Rust Programming Language for Beginners: The Ultimate
Beginner's Guide to Safe and Fast Programming"

"Rust Programming Language for Operating Systems: Build
Secure and High-Performance Operating Systems in Rust"

"Rust Programming language for Network: Build Fast,
Secure, and Scalable Systems"

"Rust Programming Language for Web Development:
Building High-Performance Web Applications and APIs"

"Rust Programming Language for Blockchains: Build
Secure, Scalable, and High-Performance Distributed
Systems"

"Rust Programming Language for Cybersecurity: Writing
Secure Code to Implementing Advanced Cryptographic
Solutions"

"Rust Programming Language for IoT: The Complete Guide
to Developing Secure and Efficient Smart Devices"

"Rust programming Language for Artificial Intelligence:
High-performance machine learning with unmatched
speed, memory safety, and concurrency from AI
innovation"

For more information, or to book an event, contact :
(Email & Website)

Book design by Jeff Stuart
Cover design by Jeff Stuart

Disclaimer

The information provided in *"Rust Programming for Web Assembly: Build Blazing-Fast, Next-Gen Web Applications"* **by Jeff Stuart** is intended solely for educational and informational purposes.

Readers are encouraged to consult qualified professionals or official documentation for specific technical, legal, or professional guidance related to their projects.

Introduction

Welcome to "**Rust Programming for Web Assembly: Build Blazing-Fast, Next-Gen Web Applications**." This Book invites you to embark on an engaging exploration of Rust and WebAssembly (Wasm), two transformative technologies that are revolutionizing web development. As web standards rapidly evolve and the demand for high-performance applications grows, mastering Rust and Wasm has become increasingly essential.

Rust is a systems programming language celebrated for its emphasis on safety and performance, providing a robust alternative to conventional web development languages. Its distinctive attributes, such as memory safety without the need for garbage collection, allow developers to produce highly efficient code while reducing the likelihood of common programming mistakes. When paired with WebAssembly—a binary instruction format engineered to execute in web browsers at speeds approaching native performance—Rust enables developers to craft applications that are not only swift but also dependable and secure.

In this Book, we will investigate how to utilize Rust to construct optimized WebAssembly modules that can greatly improve the performance of your web applications. Whether you are an experienced web developer seeking to broaden your expertise or a novice eager to explore contemporary programming paradigms, this guide will provide you with the knowledge and tools necessary for success.

Throughout the chapters, we will address key topics,

including:

Getting Started with Rust: Installation procedures, setting up your development environment, and an overview of Rust's fundamental concepts.

Diving into WebAssembly: A comprehensive understanding of what WebAssembly is, its operational mechanics, and its significance in modern web development.

Building Your First Wasm Application: A detailed, step-by-step approach to creating a simple Rust application that compiles to Wasm, allowing you to witness the process firsthand.**Optimization Techniques**: Tips and strategies for writing Rust code that maximizes performance when compiled to WebAssembly.

Chapter 1: Introduction to Rust and WebAssembly

Traditional web technologies, despite their inherent strengths, often fall short in addressing the demands of contemporary applications, particularly in fields such as gaming, data visualization, and intricate computations. Enter Rust and WebAssembly, two groundbreaking technologies that are set to transform our approach to developing and deploying web applications.

1.1 What is Rust?

Rust is a systems programming language that emphasizes speed, memory safety, and concurrency. Created by Mozilla Research, Rust has become increasingly favored by developers due to its innovative ownership model, which guarantees memory safety without the need for a garbage collector. This distinctive characteristic enables developers to produce efficient and secure code, making Rust particularly suitable for applications where performance is critical.

The syntax of Rust bears resemblance to that of C and C++, making it relatively accessible for those already acquainted with these languages. Additionally, it integrates modern programming concepts such as pattern matching, type inference, and traits, which offer robust tools for abstraction.

Rust is celebrated for its vibrant community and comprehensive ecosystem. With resources like Cargo (the Rust package manager) and Clippy (a linter), the language simplifies dependency management and encourages developers to write more idiomatic code. Moreover, Rust's focus on documentation and testing promotes a culture of high code quality and dependability.## 1.2 What is WebAssembly?

WebAssembly (often abbreviated as wasm) is a binary instruction format designed as a target for high-level programming languages. It enables execution on the web at near-native speed, making it an attractive option for performance-sensitive applications. WebAssembly is designed to run in modern web browsers as well as other environments like servers and embedded systems, providing a portable solution for developers.

The motivation behind WebAssembly is to create a safe, fast, and efficient way to run code on the web. Unlike JavaScript, which is interpreted and often has performance bottlenecks, WebAssembly provides a low-level, platform-independent compilation target that can execute quickly. It is designed to work alongside JavaScript, meaning that developers can leverage existing web technologies while tapping into the speed advantages of compiled code.

WebAssembly's security model is an crucial aspect of its design. It operates within a sandboxed environment, which isolates the execution of code, ensuring that it does not have access to the host system outside of its designated boundaries. This feature makes WebAssembly a suitable choice for running potentially untrusted code safely in web applications.

1.3 Why Combine Rust with WebAssembly?

When combining Rust with WebAssembly, developers find a potent ally for building fast and safe applications. Rust's strong emphasis on memory safety aligns perfectly with WebAssembly's design principles, creating an environment where performance does not come at the expense of reliability.

Here are some compelling reasons to combine Rust and WebAssembly:

Performance: Rust's ability to produce highly optimized machine code, coupled with WebAssembly's efficient binary format, allows applications to perform at near-native speeds in the browser.

Safety: Rust's ownership model prevents data races and provides compile-time guarantees that help eliminate a wide range of bugs. This safety persists even in the context of WebAssembly, where memory management is critical.

Portability: WebAssembly provides a universal runtime environment, enabling Rust code to run across different platforms without modification. This means a developer can write an application once and deploy it everywhere.

Interoperability: Rust and WebAssembly work seamlessly with existing web technologies. Developers can utilize WebAssembly modules alongside JavaScript, allowing them to improve performance in their applications incrementally.

Growing Ecosystem: Both Rust and WebAssembly are supported by active communities. Libraries and tools continue to be developed, further enriching this ecosystem and making it easier for developers to adopt.

1.4 Use Cases for Rust and WebAssembly

The combination of Rust and WebAssembly opens up a

wealth of opportunities across various domains:

Gaming: High-performance games can leverage the speed of WebAssembly while using Rust's capabilities for systems-level programming, leading to engaging user experiences in the browser.

Data Visualization: Applications requiring complex computations for data visualization can perform heavy lifting in Rust and deliver responsive interfaces via WebAssembly.

Scientific Simulations: Fields that rely on complex calculations, such as physics or chemistry, can utilize Rust for heavy computation, offloading the result to be displayed in a user-friendly way using WebAssembly.

File Processing: Applications that need to process large files on the client side can benefit from Rust's efficiency, reducing the load on servers and speeding up overall application performance.

As web applications grow in complexity and interactivity, the need for a robust solution that combines performance, safety, and portability becomes increasingly critical. Rust and WebAssembly together provide a formidable duo that empowers developers to push the boundaries of what is possible on the web.

The Power of Rust for Web Assembly

Alongside this revolutionary technology, the Rust programming language has risen in prominence, gleaning attention for its performance and memory safety capabilities. This chapter delves into the synergy between Rust and Web Assembly, exploring how Rust's unique features empower developers to create efficient, modern web applications.

Understanding Web Assembly

Before examining the intersection of Rust and WASM, it is crucial to understand what Web Assembly is and why it has garnered significant interest among developers. Web Assembly is a binary instruction format that allows code written in various languages to run on the web at near-native speed. Its key advantages include:

Performance: Unlike JavaScript, WASM code is compiled to a binary format that the web browser can execute more quickly, making it suitable for performance-critical applications such as games, simulations, and complex numerical computations.

Portability: WASM is designed to run on any platform with a compatible web browser, making applications accessible across devices and operating systems.

Language Agnosticism: While JavaScript has traditionally been the language of the web, WASM enables developers to leverage code written in various languages, opening the door to using languages like C, C++, and Rust for web development.

Security: WASM operates within a safe, sandboxed environment, reducing the risk of executing potentially harmful code and enhancing web security.

Why Rust?

Rust is a systems programming language designed for performance, safety, and concurrency. Its robust type system and ownership model eliminate many memory-related bugs, such as null pointer dereferences and buffer overflows, making it an ideal choice for building high-quality software. When combined with Web Assembly, Rust offers several advantages:

Performance: Rust's ability to generate highly optimized machine code translates well when targeting WASM, enhancing the performance of web applications.

Memory Safety: Rust's strong emphasis on memory safety and guarantees about nullability and data races means that developers can write safer code, reducing the risk of runtime errors often linked to memory management.

Concurrency: With support for concurrency, Rust enables developers to write applications that can efficiently utilize modern multi-core processors, enhancing performance without compromising safety.

Rich Ecosystem: The Rust ecosystem is growing rapidly, with a wide array of libraries, frameworks, and tools supporting web development. Crates like `wasm-bindgen` and `wasm-pack` simplify the process of writing and integrating Rust code into web applications.

Building a Simple WASM Application with Rust

To illustrate the power of Rust for Web Assembly, let's walk through a simple example of building a WASM application that computes the Fibonacci sequence.

Step 1: Setting Up the Environment

Before diving into the coding part, ensure you have the necessary tools installed:

Rust: Install Rust using `rustup`, which will manage your Rust installation.

wasm-pack: A CLI tool for building Rust-generated

WASM packages that you can publish to npm.

```bash
cargo install wasm-pack
```

Step 2: Creating a New Project Create a new Rust library project:

```bash
cargo new --lib fibonacci_wasm cd fibonacci_wasm
```

Step 3: Writing Rust Code

In `lib.rs`, write a simple Rust function to calculate the Fibonacci sequence:

```rust #[wasm_bindgen]
pub fn fibonacci(n: u32) -> u32 { if n <= 1 {
return n;
}
fibonacci(n - 1) + fibonacci(n - 2)
}
```

The `#[wasm_bindgen]` annotation bridges Rust and JavaScript, allowing JavaScript to call the Rust function seamlessly.

Step 4: Compiling to WASM Use `wasm-pack` to build the project:

```bash
```

```
wasm-pack build --target web
```
```

This command compiles the Rust code into a `.wasm` file, generating the necessary JavaScript bindings to interact with the compiled WASM module.

### Step 5: Integrating with HTML

Create a simple HTML file to load the WASM module:

```html
<!DOCTYPE html>
<html lang="en">
<head>
<meta charset="UTF-8">
<title>Fibonacci WASM</title>
<script type="module">
import init, { fibonacci } from './pkg/fibonacci_wasm.js';

async function run() { await init();
console.log(fibonacci(10)); // Call the Rust function
}

run();
</script>
</head>
```
```

```
<body>
<h1>Fibonacci Calculator</h1>
</body>
</html>
```

Step 6: Running the Application

Open the HTML file in a browser that supports Web Assembly, and you should see that the Fibonacci computation executes in the console.

Advanced Considerations

While building simple applications with Rust and WASM is straightforward, there are advanced topics worth exploring:

Asynchronous Programming: Rust offers powerful async features that can be utilized to handle asynchronous tasks efficiently in the web environment.

Interoperability with JavaScript: Through tooling like `wasm-bindgen`, you can interact with existing JavaScript libraries, making it easier to integrate Rust with existing web projects.

State Management: Managing application state effectively when working with WASM applications can be a challenge, requiring careful design and interaction strategies.

The combination of Rust and Web Assembly offers developers a powerful toolkit for building high-performance web applications. Rust's focus on safety and performance, together with WASM's efficiency and portability, empowers developers to push the boundaries of what is possible on the web. As the ecosystem continues to grow, adopting Rust and WASM in web development will likely become more mainstream, leading to a new era of performance-oriented, safe, and efficient web applications.

Rust for WebAssembly: Advantages, Features, and Performance

In this chapter, we will delve into the advantages and features of Rust when targeting WebAssembly, as well as its performance implications compared to traditional web technologies.

Advantages of Rust for WebAssembly ### 1. Memory Safety

One of Rust's most celebrated features is its strict memory safety guarantees. Through the ownership model, Rust eliminates the possibility of common memory-related errors such as null pointer dereferencing, buffer overflows, and data races. This safety translates exceptionally well to WebAssembly, offering developers peace of mind when running potentially unsafe code in the browser. With WebAssembly's binary format leveraging Rust's compile-time checks, developers can create applications that handle memory efficiently while ensuring reliability.

2. Concurrency

In a world where user experiences are increasingly centered around interactivity and responsiveness, concurrency is a key asset. Rust's rich concurrency models, combined with its low-level control over threads and memory, make it an excellent choice for WebAssembly applications. Developers can harness Rust's asynchronous programming capabilities to create performant web applications that can handle multiple tasks seamlessly, such as rendering graphics, processing data, and responding to user inputs, all without blocking the main thread.

3. Performance

Rust is designed for performance, making it suitable for resource-heavy applications that need to run quickly in the browser. When compiled to WebAssembly, Rust code generally runs faster than JavaScript for computation-intensive tasks due to its lower-level access to hardware and optimizations during compile time. This performance edge is particularly noticeable in applications such as games, video processing, and scientific data visualization, where efficiency is paramount.

4. Tooling and Ecosystem

Rust's rich ecosystem facilitates the development of high-quality software. With an active community and a suite of powerful tools, including the Cargo package manager and the Rustup toolchain installer, developers have everything they need at their fingertips. The integration of Rust with WebAssembly is seamless, thanks to libraries like `wasm-bindgen`, which allows Rust code to interact naturally with JavaScript and the Web APIs, bridging the gap between native performance and web standards.

Features of Rust in WebAssembly Development ### 1. Seamless Interoperability with JavaScript

Rust's ability to interoperate with JavaScript is one of its most compelling features when targeting WebAssembly. Via libraries like `wasm-bindgen`, developers can easily expose Rust functions to JavaScript and invoke JavaScript from Rust. This bidirectional communication opens up a plethora of possibilities, allowing developers to write performance-critical sections of their applications in Rust while leveraging the rich ecosystem of JavaScript libraries and frameworks. ### 2. Modularity and Reusability

Rust encourages modular programming practices through its package manager, Cargo, which allows for the creation of reusable libraries. When compiling to WebAssembly, these modules can be packaged into smaller, efficient units that can be imported into larger applications seamlessly. This modular architecture not only enhances code maintainability but also encourages the sharing of libraries across projects, further fostering innovation within the Rust and WebAssembly community.

3. Advanced Optimizations

The Rust compiler (rustc) employs advanced optimizations to ensure that the output code, when compiled to WebAssembly, runs efficiently within web environments. Features such as inlining, dead code elimination, and aggressive type inference mean that developers can write clear, expressive code without worrying about the performance implications. As a result, Rust's compiler is capable of producing highly optimized WebAssembly output with minimal effort from the developer.

Performance Implications

1. Benchmarking and Real-World Examples

The performance of Rust-compiled WebAssembly applications can be significantly better than that of traditional JavaScript implementations, especially in scenarios involving heavy computation. Benchmarks have shown that tasks involving complex algorithms, data manipulation, and real-time processing can outperform pure JavaScript implementations by significant margins. For instance, projects such as `wasm- bindgen` and libraries like `yew` have facilitated the creation of applications that demonstrate this performance leap effectively.

2. Size Considerations

While Rust offers excellent performance, there are considerations regarding the size of the resulting WebAssembly binaries. Rust's standard library and certain features can add overhead to the compiled output, making the binary larger compared to more lightweight implementations. However, developers can mitigate this concern through various techniques, such as using the `--release` flag to enable optimizations that produce smaller binaries and employing features like code splitting to load necessary parts of the application as needed.

3. Future Outlook

As the WebAssembly ecosystem continues to evolve, Rust's role within it is growing stronger. The ongoing development of Rust tooling and libraries for WebAssembly will likely revolutionize how developers approach web applications, enabling even more sophisticated uses of Rust's features. With increasing support from browser vendors and a robust community backing the technology, the future looks bright for Rust and WebAssembly.

With its powerful features and excellent tooling, developers can harness the best of both worlds—the performance of low-level programming and the accessibility of modern web development.

Chapter 2: Getting Started with Rust and WebAssembly Toolchains

Rust's combination of performance, memory safety, and modern language features make it an excellent choice for compiling to WebAssembly, which allows you to run code in web browsers with near-native performance. To kick things off, we will cover how to set up your environment and the essential toolchains necessary for building WebAssembly applications with Rust.

2.1 Prerequisites

Before we dive into the setup process, make sure you have the following prerequisites:

A Working Rust Installation: If you haven't installed Rust yet, you can do so by using the Rustup installer, which manages Rust versions and associated tools. To install Rust, run:

```bash
curl --proto '=https' --tlsv1.2 -sSf https://sh.rustup.rs | sh
```

Follow the on-screen prompts to complete the installation. After installation, ensure that your `PATH` is set up correctly by running:

```bash
source $HOME/.cargo/env
```

The Latest Version of Cargo: Cargo, Rust's official package manager and build system, comes bundled with

Rust. You can verify that Cargo is installed by executing:

```bash
cargo --version
```

WebAssembly Target: To compile Rust code into WebAssembly, you need to add the appropriate target. You can do this easily with the following command:

```bash
rustup target add wasm32-unknown-unknown
```

2.2 Setting Up a New Rust Project

Now that you've ensured a complete Rust setup, let's create a new Rust project that will compile to WebAssembly.

Create a New Project: Use Cargo to create a new project by executing:

```bash
cargo new rust_wasm_project cd rust_wasm_project
```

Modify `Cargo.toml`: Open the `Cargo.toml` file and update it to include the necessary dependencies and ensure that the output is suitable for WebAssembly. Below is an example configuration:

```toml
[package]
name = "rust_wasm_project" version = "0.1.0"
```

```
edition = "2021"
[lib]
crate-type = ["cdylib"]
[dependencies]
wasm-bindgen = "0.2"
```

2.3 Writing Your First WebAssembly Function

Now that we have set up our project, let's write a simple function that we will compile into WebAssembly.

Modify `src/lib.rs`: Open the `src/lib.rs` file and replace its contents with the following code:

```rust
use wasm_bindgen::prelude::*;

#[wasm_bindgen]

pub fn greet(name: &str) -> String { format!("Hello, {}!",
name)

}
```

This code defines a function `greet` that takes a string parameter and returns a greeting message as a string. The `#[wasm_bindgen]` macro exposes this function to JavaScript, enabling interaction with the WebAssembly module.

2.4 Compiling to WebAssembly

Once you've written your function, it's time to compile your project to WebAssembly.

Compile the Project: Execute the following command to build your project for the WebAssembly target:

```bash
cargo build --target wasm32-unknown-unknown --release
```

This command builds your project in release mode, resulting in a `.wasm` file generated in the

`target/wasm32-unknown-unknown/release` directory.
2.5 Setting Up a JavaScript Environment

To utilize the WebAssembly module in a web application, you will need to set up a simple HTML and JavaScript environment.

Create an HTML File: In the root of your project, create an `index.html` file and include the following content:

```html
<!DOCTYPE html>
<html lang="en">
<head>
<meta charset="UTF-8">
<meta name="viewport" content="width=device-width, initial-scale=1.0">
<title>Rust + WebAssembly</title>
</head>
<body>
<h1>Rust and WebAssembly</h1>
```

```html
<input id="name-input" type="text" placeholder="Enter your name">
<button id="greet-button">Greet</button>
<p id="greeting"></p>
<script type="module">
import init, { greet } from './target/wasm32-unknown-unknown/release/rust_wasm_project.js'; async function run() {
await init();
document.getElementById('greet-button').onclick = () => { const name = document.getElementById('name-input').value; const greeting = greet(name); document.getElementById('greeting').textContent = greeting;
};
}
run();
</script>
</body>
</html>
```

This file creates a simple user interface where users can input their names and see a greeting generated by our WebAssembly function.

2.6 Running Your Project

To see your project in action, follow these steps:

Start a Web Server: You can use any basic web server, but for simplicity, we can use `http-server` from npm. If you don't have it installed, you can do so with:

```bash
npm install -g http-server
```

Serve Your Files: Run the following command to serve your project:

```bash
http-server .
```

Open in Browser: Navigate to the URL provided by the web server (usually `http://localhost:8080`) and test your application by entering a name and clicking the "Greet" button.

From setting up your environment, writing your first Rust function, to creating a simple web application interface, you now have a foundational understanding of the Rust and WebAssembly toolchains.

Setting Up Your Development Environment: Rust, wasm-pack, and cargo

The allure of WebAssembly (Wasm) lies in its promise of enabling high-performance applications in the browser, allowing developers to write code in languages like Rust and deploy it seamlessly on the web. However, before diving into the intricacies of building WebAssembly modules, it's essential to lay down a solid foundation by setting up your development environment. In this chapter, we'll guide you through installing Rust, configuring `wasm-pack`, and utilizing `Cargo` to streamline your coding experience.

1. Installing Rust

Rust is a systems programming language focused on speed, memory safety, and parallelism. To begin, you'll want to install Rust, which comes packaged with a toolchain that makes developing Rust applications straightforward.

Step 1: Install Rustup

The recommended way to install Rust is through `rustup`, a tool that manages Rust versions and associated tools. To install, open your terminal and execute the following command:

```bash
curl --proto '=https' --tlsv1.2 -sSf https://sh.rustup.rs | sh
```

This command downloads a script that installs `rustup`. You'll be prompted to proceed with the installation; press **Enter** to continue.

Step 2: Configure Your Path

Once installed, it's crucial to configure your shell's path. The installation script modifies your shell profile file, typically located at `~/.profile`, `~/.bashrc`, or `~/.zshrc`. Restart your terminal or run:

```bash
source $HOME/.cargo/env
```

Step 3: Verify the Installation

To ensure Rust is installed correctly, run:

```bash
rustc --version
```

This command should display the installed version of Rust, confirming the installation was a success. ## 2. Setting Up wasm-pack

`wasm-pack` is a tool that facilitates building Rust-generated WebAssembly packages. It packages your Rust code, generates the necessary JavaScript bindings, and can also publish packages to the npm registry.

Step 1: Install wasm-pack

To install `wasm-pack`, you can use `cargo`, Rust's package manager. In your terminal, run:

```bash
cargo install wasm-pack
```

This command downloads and compiles `wasm-pack`. Once completed, verify the installation:

```bash
wasm-pack --version
```

```
```

Step 2: Check for Updates

As with most development tools, keeping `wasm-pack` up to date is essential. To check for and install updates, run:

```bash

cargo install --force wasm-pack

```

3. Creating a New Rust Project with Cargo

With Rust and `wasm-pack` set up, the next step is to create a new Rust project using `Cargo`, Rust's built-in package manager and build system.

Step 1: Create Your Project

To create a new Rust project, execute the following command, replacing `your_project_name` with your desired project name:

```bash

cargo new your_project_name --lib

```

The `--lib` flag indicates that you'll build a library (which is useful for creating a WebAssembly module). ### Step 2: Navigate to Your Project Directory

Change into your project directory:

```bash

cd your_project_name

```

Step 3: Modify the Cargo.toml File

Open the `Cargo.toml` file created in your project directory. You need to add dependencies that enable WebAssembly support. Below is an example of what your `Cargo.toml` might look like:

```toml
[package]

name = "your_project_name"

version = "0.1.0"

edition = "2021"

[lib]

crate-type = ["cdylib"]

[dependencies]

wasm-bindgen = "0.2"
```

The `crate-type = ["cdylib"]` line tells Rust to compile your project as a dynamic library suitable for WebAssembly.

4. Writing Your First Rust Function

Let's create a basic Rust function that will be compiled to WebAssembly. Open the `src/lib.rs` file and add the following code:

```rust
use wasm_bindgen::prelude::*;

#[wasm_bindgen]

pub fn greet(name: &str) -> String { format!("Hello, {}!",
name)
```

}
```
```

This simple function takes a string input and returns a greeting. ## 5. Building Your WebAssembly Module

With your function defined, it's time to compile it into a WebAssembly module using `wasm-pack`. ### Step 1: Build the Project

In your project directory, run:

```bash

wasm-pack build

```

This command compiles your Rust code into WebAssembly and generates the necessary bindings. By default, it creates an output directory named `pkg`, which contains the compiled `.wasm` file along with a JavaScript file for interfacing with the WebAssembly module.

Step 2: Verify the Output

Navigate to the `pkg` directory to see the output files. You should find your `.wasm` file and `.js` file, which you can use in your web applications.

In this chapter, we explored the fundamental steps needed to set up a development environment for Rust and WebAssembly using `wasm-pack` and `Cargo`. With Rust installed, `wasm-pack` at your disposal, and a new project created, you are now prepared to begin building high-performance WebAssembly applications.

Installing and Configuring Tools for Seamless WebAssembly Development

This chapter provides a step-by-step guide on setting up your environment for seamless WebAssembly development, including essential tools, installation instructions, and configuration tips.

1. Understanding the WebAssembly Ecosystem

Before diving into installations, it's important to familiarize yourself with the ecosystem surrounding WebAssembly. While you can compile code from various programming languages into WebAssembly, the most commonly used languages include C, C++, Rust, and AssemblyScript. Each of these languages has associated toolchains and libraries that need to be installed.

2. Prerequisites

2.1 Operating System

WebAssembly development can be done on various operating systems, including:

Windows

macOS

Linux

Ensure that your operating system is up to date. Many tools will require a version of Node.js, so install that first if you haven't done so.

2.2 Compilation Tools

Depending on your chosen programming language, install the following tools:

- **For C/C++**:

Emscripten: This is the primary toolchain for compiling C and C++ code to WebAssembly.

For Rust:

Rustup: The Rust toolchain manager.

wasm-bindgen: A library that facilitates high-level interactions between WebAssembly and JavaScript.

For AssemblyScript:

AssemblyScript Compiler: A TypeScript-like language that compiles to WebAssembly. ## 3. Installing Essential Tools

3.1 Emscripten for C/C++

Install Emscripten:

You can obtain Emscripten via the Emscripten SDK. Follow these steps:

```bash
git clone https://github.com/emscripten-core/emsdk.git
cd emsdk
./emsdk install latest
./emsdk activate latest
```

Configure Environment Variables:

Run the following command to set up the environment variables:

```bash
```

source ./emsdk_env.sh
```

### 3.2 Rust Toolchain
**Install Rustup**:
Use the following command to install Rustup:
```bash
curl --proto '=https' --tlsv1.2 -sSf https://sh.rustup.rs | sh
```

Add the WebAssembly target:
Once Rust is installed, execute:
```bash
rustup target add wasm32-unknown-unknown
```

Install wasm-bindgen:
To install the `wasm-bindgen` CLI, run:
```bash
cargo install wasm-bindgen-cli
```

3.3 AssemblyScript
Install Node.js:
First, make sure Node.js and npm are installed. Use:
```bash
npm install -g assemblyscript

```
```

Set Up a New Project:

Create a new project directory and use AssemblyScript to scaffold it:

```bash
npx asinit my-assemblyscript-project cd my-assemblyscript-project

npm install
```

4. Integrated Development Environment (IDE)

Choosing the right IDE can significantly enhance your development experience. Here are some recommended IDEs:

Visual Studio Code: A popular choice among web developers; offers several extensions for WebAssembly, including ones for Rust and Emscripten.

Clion: A more heavy-duty IDE suited for C/C++ development, which can also work well with Emscripten.

IntelliJ IDEA: With plugins for supporting various languages, IntelliJ IDEA can be an excellent choice for mixed-language projects.

Regardless of the IDE, ensure that you enable linting, syntax highlighting, and relevant plugins for WebAssembly development.

5. Setting Up a Local Server

To test your WebAssembly applications locally:

Using Node.js:

Install `http-server` globally:

```bash
npm install -g http-server
```

- Start the server in your project directory:

```bash
http-server .
```

Using Python (as an alternative):

If you have Python installed, you can start a simple HTTP server:

```bash
python3 -m http.server
```

6. Testing Your Setup

After installing and configuring your tools, it's time to test your setup. Create a simple WebAssembly project in your chosen language. For example, using Rust, you could create a basic "Hello, World!" program:

```rust
// src/lib.rs #[no_mangle]
pub extern "C" fn greet() {
// Function logic here
```

```
}
```
```
` ` `
```

Build the project with the appropriate command (such as `wasm-pack build` for Rust projects) and run your local server. Open your browser and navigate to your project directory to ensure that everything works as expected.

By following the steps outlined in this chapter, you have successfully set up and configured a development environment tailored for WebAssembly. As you continue exploring this technology, remember that the tools and configurations can vary based on your specific use cases and the languages you choose to work with.

With the right environment in place, you are now equipped to embark on your WebAssembly development journey.

Chapter 3: The Fundamentals of Rust Programming

In this chapter, we will delve into the foundational aspects of Rust, including its syntax, data types, ownership principles, and control flow constructs. By the end of this chapter, you will have a solid understanding of the essential building blocks of Rust programming.

3.1 Getting Started with Rust

Before diving into the intricacies of Rust programming, ensure you have Rust installed on your machine. The recommended way to install Rust is through `rustup`, a toolchain installer for Rust. Once installed, you can create a new Rust project with the following commands:

```bash
cargo new my_project cd my_project
```

This will create a new directory named `my_project` containing a basic Rust project structure, including a

`Cargo.toml` file for dependency management and a `src/main.rs` file, which serves as the entry point for your application.

3.2 Basic Syntax

Rust's syntax is C-like, making it relatively easy for programmers familiar with C, C++, or Java to pick up. Let's start with a simple "Hello, World!" program:

```rust
fn main() {
```

```
println!("Hello, World!");
}
```

3.2.1 Functions

Functions in Rust are defined using the `fn` keyword, followed by the function name and a pair of parentheses containing parameters. The return type is specified after an arrow (`->`). If a function doesn't return a value, it defaults to returning an empty tuple `()`.

Here's an example of a function that takes two integers and returns their sum:

```rust
fn add(a: i32, b: i32) -> i32 {
    a + b // No need for a return statement; the last expression is returned
}
```

3.2.2 Variables and Data Types

Rust is statically typed, meaning that the type of a variable must be known at compile time. Variables are immutable by default, and you can declare a mutable variable using the `mut` keyword:

```rust
let x = 5; // Immutable variable

let mut y = 10; // Mutable variable y += 5; // Now y equals 15
```

```
```

Rust provides several built-in data types:

Scalar Types: Such as integers (`i32`, `u32`, `f64`), booleans (`bool`), and characters (`char`).

Compound Types: Such as tuples and arrays. Example of a tuple:

```rust
let tuple: (i32, f64, char) = (500, 6.4, 'z'); let (x, y, z) = tuple; // Destructuring a tuple
```

Example of an array:

```rust
let arr: [i32; 5] = [1, 2, 3, 4, 5]; // An array of 5 integers
```

3.3 Ownership and Borrowing

One of the hallmarks of Rust is its ownership model, which ensures memory safety without a garbage collector. The core principles of this model are:

3.3.1 Ownership

Each value in Rust has a variable that is its "owner."

A value can only have one owner at a time.

When the owner goes out of scope, Rust automatically cleans up (drops) the value. Here's an example:

```rust
{
```

```
let s1 = String::from("Hello");

let s2 = s1; // s1 is no longer valid; ownership is
transferred to s2

}
```
` ` `

3.3.2 Borrowing

Instead of transferring ownership, you can reference a value using borrowing. Rust allows both immutable and mutable borrowing:

Immutable Borrowing: You cannot change the value while it is borrowed.

` ` `rust

```
let s = String::from("Hello"); let r = &s; // Immutable
borrow
```
` ` `

Mutable Borrowing: Allows you to change the borrowed value but can only have one mutable reference at a time.

` ` `rust

```
let mut s = String::from("Hello"); let r = &mut s; //
Mutable borrow r.push_str(", World!");
```
` ` `

3.4 Control Flow

Control flow constructs in Rust include `if` statements, loops, and match statements. ### 3.4.1 If Statements

Rust's `if` statements work similarly to other languages,

allowing you to execute code based on a conditional expression:

```rust
let number = 6;

if number % 2 == 0 { println!("Even");
} else { println!("Odd");
}
```

3.4.2 Loops

Rust provides three types of loops: `loop`, `while`, and `for`.

Loop: An infinite loop. Use `break` to exit the loop.

```rust
loop {
println!("This will loop forever until we break out!");
break; // Exiting the loop
}
```

While Loop: Executes as long as a condition is true.

```rust
let mut count = 0; while count < 5 {
println!("Count is: {}", count); count += 1;
}
```

For Loop: Iterates over a range or collection.

```rust
for i in 0..5 { println!("i is: {}", i);
}
```

3.4.3 Match Statement

The `match` statement is a powerful control flow operator in Rust that allows pattern matching.

```rust
let number = 1;
match number {
1 => println!("One"),
2 => println!("Two"),
_ => println!("Other"), // The catch-all case
}
```

We explored core concepts such as basic syntax, variables, data types, the ownership model, and control flow constructs. These fundamentals are crucial as you continue your journey into more advanced topics like concurrency, traits, and error handling in Rust. With this knowledge, you are now prepared to start building programs with Rust's unique capabilities that prioritize memory safety and performance.

Core Syntax and Constructs of Rust: Variables, Types, and Functions

This chapter will delve deep into the core syntax and constructs of Rust, focusing on variables, types, and functions. Understanding these fundamental elements is crucial for any developer looking to harness the power of Rust and build robust software applications.

1. Variables in Rust

In Rust, a variable is a fundamental entity used to store data. Unlike many other programming languages, Rust enforces strict rules around variable mutability and ownership, ensuring memory safety and concurrent programming without the fear of data races.

1.1 Variable Binding and Mutability

By default, variables in Rust are immutable, which means once a variable is assigned a value, it cannot be changed. To create a mutable variable, the `mut` keyword is used. Here's how it works:

```rust
fn main() {

let x = 5; // Immutable variable

// x = 10; // This will cause a compilation error

let mut y = 10; // Mutable variable y = 15; // This is allowed println!("The value of y is: {}", y);

}
```

1.2 Shadowing

Rust allows a feature called shadowing, where a new variable can take the place of a previously declared one in the same scope. This provides flexibility and clarity. Shadowing can also change the type of the variable:

```rust
fn main() { let x = 5;

let x = x + 1; // x is now 6

{

let x = x * 2; // Shadowing with a new scope
println!("Inner x: {}", x); // Prints 12

}

println!("Outer x: {}", x); // Prints 6

}
```

2. Types in Rust

Rust is a statically typed language, meaning all variable types must be known at compile time. This feature helps catch many common bugs early in the development process.

2.1 Scalar Types

Rust has several built-in scalar types, including integers, floating-point numbers, booleans, and characters:

Integers: Rust supports both signed and unsigned integers of various sizes (`i8`, `i16`, `i32`, `i64`,

`i128`, `isize`, `u8`, `u16`, `u32`, `u64`, `u128`,

`usize`).

Floating-point numbers: It offers `f32` and `f64`, representing 32-bit and 64-bit floating-point numbers, respectively.

Boolean: The `bool` type can hold either `true` or `false`.

Character: The `char` type represents a single Unicode character.

```rust
fn main() {

let int_num: i32 = 42; // Signed integer

let float_num: f64 = 3.14; // Floating-point number let boolean: bool = true; // Boolean

let character: char = 'A'; // Character

println!("Integer: {}, Float: {}, Boolean: {}, Character: {}", int_num, float_num, boolean, character);

}
```

2.2 Compound Types

Compound types in Rust allow you to group multiple values into a single entity. Rust includes two primary compound types: tuples and arrays.

Tuples: A tuple can hold a fixed number of elements of varying types.

```rust
fn main() {
```

```rust
let person: (&str, i32) = ("Alice", 30); println!("Name: {},
Age: {}", person.0, person.1);
}
```

Arrays: Arrays store elements of the same type in a fixed-size structure.

```rust
fn main() {
let numbers: [i32; 5] = [1, 2, 3, 4, 5]; for number in
&numbers {
println!("{}", number);
}
}
```

3. Functions in Rust

Functions are a core building block in Rust, encapsulating behavior that can be invoked with a name. They improve code readability and reusability.

3.1 Function Syntax

In Rust, functions are declared using the `fn` keyword, followed by the function name, parameters, and return type. Here's a simple function example:

```rust
fn add(a: i32, b: i32) -> i32 { a + b
```

```
}
fn main() {
let sum = add(3, 5); println!("Sum: {}", sum);
}
```
```

### 3.2 Function Parameters and Return Types

Function parameters in Rust are explicitly typed. The return type follows the parameter list after an arrow (`->`). If the function returns nothing, it uses the `()` type, which signifies an empty tuple:

```rust
fn greet(name: &str) -> () { println!("Hello, {}!", name);
}
```
```

3.3 Closures

Rust supports first-class functions and closures, allowing functions to be treated as variables. A closure can capture its environment, making it a powerful feature for functional programming.

```rust
fn main() {
let add = |x: i32, y: i32| x + y; // Closure let result = add(10, 5);
println!("Closure Result: {}", result);
}
```

```

```

This chapter has introduced the core syntax and constructs of Rust, emphasizing variables, types, and functions. Understanding these elements is vital for leveraging Rust's features effectively and safely.

Memory Safety, Ownership, and Borrowing: Key Concepts for Beginners

This chapter will introduce these fundamental concepts, providing a solid foundation for understanding how Rust manages memory and prevents common bugs found in other languages.

1. Memory Safety

Memory safety is a critical aspect of programming, particularly in systems programming where direct memory manipulation is common. In languages like C and C++, it's easy to encounter issues such as null pointer dereferencing, buffer overflows, or use-after-free errors. Rust addresses these problems at compile time through its ownership model, ensuring that programs are safe from these types of errors before they run.

Memory safety in Rust is guaranteed through several key principles:

No Use-After-Free: A piece of memory cannot be accessed if it's been freed. In Rust, once a value goes out of scope, it's automatically deallocated, and any subsequent access will not compile.

No Dangling References: Rust guarantees that references always point to valid memory. When a value is moved, any references to that value become invalid.

No Data Races: The compiler's borrowing rules ensure that data is either mutable or shared, but never both at the same time. This prevents simultaneous access issues that lead to data races, a common problem in multithreading scenarios.

2. Ownership

At the heart of Rust's memory management is the concept of ownership. Every value in Rust has a single "owner," which is the variable that holds that value. The rules of ownership dictate how memory is allocated, accessed, and deallocated:

Each value has a single owner: When an owner goes out of scope, Rust automatically cleans up the memory associated with that value.

Ownership can be transferred: When you assign a value from one variable to another, the original variable no longer owns the value (this is known as moving the value). This prevents a situation where two variables own the same resource and can lead to double frees.

Here's a basic example to illustrate ownership:

```rust
fn main() {
let s1 = String::from("Hello"); // s1 is the owner of the
String. let s2 = s1; // Ownership of the String is moved to
s2.
```

```
// println!("{}", s1); // This would cause a compile-time
error. println!("{}", s2); // Correctly prints "Hello".

}
```

In this example, when we assign `s1` to `s2`, `s1` loses its ownership of the string. Any attempt to use `s1` afterwards will result in a compile error, preventing potential runtime issues.

3. The Borrowing Mechanism

While ownership ensures that each value has a single owner, Rust also provides a way to "borrow" values temporarily. Borrowing allows us to refer to a value without taking ownership of it, enabling the reuse of data without risk of memory errors.

There are two types of borrowing: immutable and mutable. ### Immutable Borrowing

You can have multiple immutable references to a value at the same time. This means that you can read data from a variable but not modify it:

```rust
fn main() {

let s = String::from("Hello");

let r1 = &s; // Immutable borrow

let r2 = &s; // Another immutable borrow

println!("{} and {}", r1, r2);

}
```

```
```

In the example above, both `r1` and `r2` borrow `s` immutably, allowing us to read the value without changing it.

Mutable Borrowing

Mutable borrowing allows a single mutable reference to a value, which means you can change the value. However, while a value is mutably borrowed, you cannot have any immutable references to it:

```rust
fn main() {

let mut s = String::from("Hello"); let r = &mut s; // Mutable borrow

r.push_str(", world!"); // Modify the borrowed value println!("{}", r); // Prints "Hello, world!"

}
```

In this case, the mutable reference `r` allows us to modify the string. However, if we tried to borrow `s` immutably while `r` exists, the code would fail to compile:

```rust
let r1 = &s; // This would cause a compile-time error if r is still in use.
```

4. Lifetimes

An advanced concept tied closely to ownership and

borrowing is lifetimes. Rust uses lifetimes to ensure that references are valid as long as they're being used. This prevents dangling references and enforces the rules of borrowing.

While lifetimes can be initially perplexing, they are often not explicit in simpler programs due to Rust's ability to infer them. However, when functions take references as parameters or return references, Rust requires explicit lifetime annotations to ensure validity.

Here's an example:

```rust
fn long_lived<'a>(s: &'a str) -> &'a str { s
}
```

In this function, the lifetimes `'a` show that the returned reference will live at least as long as the input reference. This ensures that the caller has a valid reference when they use the return value.

These concepts provide a powerful system that prevents many common programming errors, fostering safer and more efficient code. As you continue your journey in Rust, remember that while these concepts may seem daunting at first, they offer a framework that ultimately leads to more reliable software. Practice and experimentation are key—so dive into writing Rust code and see these principles in action!

Chapter 4: Building Your First Rust-to-WebAssembly Project

Rust has gained immense popularity for its performance and safety features, while WebAssembly provides a way to run code written in languages other than JavaScript on the web. Together, they complement each other beautifully, allowing developers to create high-performance web applications. By the end of this chapter, you'll have a foundational understanding of how to create and deploy a simple Rust-to- WebAssembly project.

4.1 Prerequisites

Before we dive into the project, make sure you have the following tools installed on your system:

Rust: You can install Rust using [rustup](https://rustup.rs/). This will set up Rust and Cargo (Rust's package manager).

wasm-pack: This tool helps you build, package, and publish Rust-generated WebAssembly. You can install it via Cargo by running:

```bash

cargo install wasm-pack

```

Node.js (optional): For local development, having Node.js and npm installed will help you run a simple development server. If you do not have Node.js installed, you can download it from nodejs.org.

A Code Editor: While you can use any text editor, you

56

might find it helpful to use an editor that supports Rust, such as Visual Studio Code with the Rust extension.

4.2 Creating Your First Rust Project Let's create a new Rust project:

Open your terminal and create a new directory for your project:

```bash
mkdir rust_wasm_demo cd rust_wasm_demo
```

Next, create a new Rust package using Cargo. This package will hold our WebAssembly code:

```bash
cargo new --lib rust_wasm cd rust_wasm
```

Now that we have a new Rust library, we need to modify the `Cargo.toml` file to include the necessary dependencies for working with WebAssembly. Open `Cargo.toml` and modify it to look like this:

```toml
[package]
name = "rust_wasm" version = "0.1.0"
edition = "2021"
[lib]
crate-type = ["cdylib"]
[dependencies]
wasm-bindgen = "0.2"
```

```
```

The `wasm-bindgen` crate is essential for interoperate between JavaScript and Rust, allowing us to call Rust functions from JavaScript.

4.3 Writing Some Rust Code

Let's write some simple Rust code that we'll compile to WebAssembly. Open the `src/lib.rs` file and replace its contents with the following code:

```rust
use wasm_bindgen::prelude::*;

#[wasm_bindgen]

pub fn greet(name: &str) -> String { format!("Hello, {}!", name)

}
```

In this code snippet, we define a simple function `greet` that takes a name as input and returns a greeting message.

4.4 Compiling to WebAssembly

Now it's time to compile our code to WebAssembly. Run the following command to do this:

```bash
wasm-pack build --target web
```

This command compiles your Rust code into a `.wasm` file and generates the bindings needed for JavaScript. You will see a new directory called `pkg` containing the compiled files.

4.5 Setting Up a Simple Web Page

Next, create an HTML file to load our WebAssembly module. Create a new directory called `www`:

```bash
mkdir www
cd www
```

Inside the `www` directory, create an `index.html` file with the following content:

```html
<!DOCTYPE html>
<html lang="en">
<head>
<meta charset="UTF-8">
<meta name="viewport" content="width=device-width, initial-scale=1.0">
<title>Rust WASM Demo</title>
<script type="module">
import init, { greet } from '../pkg/rust_wasm.js';

async function run() { await init();

const name = prompt("Enter your name:"); const message = greet(name);

document.getElementById("output").innerText      = message;
}
```

```
run();
</script>
</head>
<body>
<h1>Rust and WebAssembly</h1>
<div id="output"></div>
</body>
</html>
```
```

This HTML file will load the WebAssembly binary and call the `greet` function, which will display the greeting message in the web browser.

## 4.6 Serving Your Application

To see your app in action, you need to serve the HTML file using a web server. If you have Node.js installed, you can create your server using the `http-server` package. If you don't have it, you can install it via npm:

```bash
npm install -g http-server
```

Then navigate back to the root of your project and run:

```bash
http-server www
```

Open your browser and go to `http://localhost:8080`.
```

You should be greeted with a prompt asking for your name. Upon entering your name, you should see a greeting displayed on the page.

This chapter covered the basics, including setting up your development environment, writing Rust code, compiling it to WebAssembly, and serving it as a web application. This is just the beginning—there's much more you can do with Rust and WebAssembly, including creating complex applications that utilize web APIs or integrating with existing JavaScript libraries.

Writing a Basic Rust Program and Compiling to WebAssembly

WebAssembly (often abbreviated as wasm) is a binary instruction format designed for safe, portable, and efficient execution on the web. It enables developers to run code written in languages like Rust in the browser, providing near-native performance.

In this chapter, we will guide you through the steps to write a basic Rust program and compile it to WebAssembly. By the end of this chapter, you will have a foundational understanding of how to create a Rust project, the basics of WebAssembly, and how to run your compiled code in a web environment.

Setting Up Your Environment

Before we begin, make sure that you have the following tools installed on your machine:

Rust: If you haven't installed Rust yet, you can do so by using `rustup`, the Rust toolchain installer. Run the following command in your terminal:

```bash
curl --proto '=https' --tlsv1.2 -sSf https://sh.rustup.rs | sh
```

Follow the on-screen instructions to complete the installation.

wasm-pack: This tool simplifies the process of building and packaging Rust-generated WebAssembly. You can install it with:

```bash
cargo install wasm-pack
```

A Web server: For serving our WebAssembly application, we can use a simple HTTP server. You can use tools like `http-server`, `live-server`, or even the built-in `python -m http.server`. If you don't have one installed, you can use `npm` to install `http-server`:

```bash
npm install --global http-server
```

Creating a Basic Rust Program

Let's start by creating a new Rust project. Open your terminal and run the following commands:

```bash
cargo new rust_to_wasm cd rust_to_wasm
```

This will create a new directory called `rust_to_wasm` with the necessary project structure. The main source files are located in the `src` directory, particularly in a file named `main.rs`.

Next, we need to modify our project so that it can compile to WebAssembly. First, we'll create a new library file instead of a binary file.

Modifying the Project Structure

Change the project type: Open `Cargo.toml` and modify it to indicate that we are creating a library. Replace the content with the following:

```toml
[package]
name = "rust_to_wasm" version = "0.1.0"
edition = "2021"
[lib]
crate-type = ["cdylib"]
[dependencies]
wasm-bindgen = "0.2"
```

Creating the WebAssembly Module: In the `src` directory, remove the `main.rs` file and create a new file called `lib.rs`. Inside `lib.rs`, add the following Rust code:

```rust
use wasm_bindgen::prelude::*;
#[wasm_bindgen]
```

63

```rust
pub fn greet(name: &str) -> String { format!("Hello, {}!",
name)
}
```

In the code above, we define a simple function `greet` that takes a string (the name) and returns a greeting message.

Compiling to WebAssembly

Now that we have our Rust code ready, it's time to compile it to WebAssembly. In your terminal, run the following command:

```bash
wasm-pack build --target web
```

This command compiles the Rust code into a WebAssembly binary and generates the necessary JavaScript bindings to interact with the WebAssembly module. It will create a new `pkg` directory which contains everything you need to integrate it into a web application.

Creating an HTML Interface

Next, we'll create a simple HTML file to load our WebAssembly module and call the `greet` function.

Inside the `rust_to_wasm` directory, create an `index.html` file:

```html
```

```html
<!DOCTYPE html>
<html>
<head>
<title>Rust to WebAssembly</title>
<script type="module">
import init, { greet } from './pkg/rust_to_wasm.js';
async function run() {
await init(); // Initialize the WebAssembly module const greeting = greet("World");
document.getElementById('greeting').innerText         = greeting;
}
run();
</script>
</head>
<body>
<h1 id="greeting">Loading...</h1>
</body>
</html>
```
```

In this HTML file, we import the generated WebAssembly JavaScript bindings, initialize the module, and call the `greet` function. The result is displayed in a `<h1>` element.

## Running the Application
```

Now that everything is set up, it's time to run our application. In the terminal, execute the following command inside the project directory:

```bash
http-server
```

By default, `http-server` will serve the content on `http://localhost:8080`. Open this URL in your web browser, and you should see "Hello, World!" displayed on the page.

Running WebAssembly in the Browser with JavaScript Integration

WebAssembly is not a replacement for JavaScript; rather, it complements it by allowing developers to write performance-critical code in languages like Rust, C, and C++. In this chapter, we will explore how to compile Rust code into WebAssembly and interact with it seamlessly using JavaScript.

Why Rust for WebAssembly?

Rust has emerged as a popular choice for WebAssembly development due to its memory safety guarantees, zero-cost abstractions, and strong type system. It enables developers to write concurrent code without fear of data races or memory leaks, making it ideal for performance-sensitive applications. Additionally, Rust's package manager, Cargo, provides an easy way to manage dependencies and build WebAssembly modules.

Setting Up the Environment

Before we dive into coding, we need to set up our environment. Here's what you'll need:

Rust: Make sure you have Rust installed. You can do this by following the instructions on the [official Rust website](https://www.rust-lang.org/).

wasm-pack: This is a tool that simplifies the process of building and packaging Rust code to be used as WebAssembly. Install it by running the following command in your terminal:

```bash
cargo install wasm-pack
```

Node.js and npm: These are needed for managing JavaScript dependencies. You can download them from the [official Node.js website](https://nodejs.org/).

A code editor: Any text editor or IDE that supports Rust and JavaScript will do. Popular choices include Visual Studio Code and IntelliJ IDEA.

Creating a New Rust Project

We'll begin by creating a new Rust project using Cargo. Open your terminal and execute the following commands:

```bash
cargo new wasm_example cd wasm_example
```

This creates a new directory called `wasm_example` with a simple Rust project initialized inside. ## Writing Rust Code

Next, we need to modify our Rust project to include some code that can be compiled to WebAssembly. Open `Cargo.toml` in your project directory and add the following dependencies:

```toml [lib]
crate-type = ["cdylib"]
[dependencies]
wasm-bindgen = "0.2.79"  # or the latest version
```

Now, let's write a simple function in `src/lib.rs` that we want to expose to JavaScript. This function will take two numbers and return their sum:

```rust
use wasm_bindgen::prelude::*;

#[wasm_bindgen]
pub fn add(a: i32, b: i32) -> i32 { a + b
}
```

The `#[wasm_bindgen]` attribute allows us to integrate with JavaScript. ## Compiling to WebAssembly

With our Rust code ready, let's compile it to WebAssembly. Run the following command in your terminal:

```bash
```

```
wasm-pack build --target web
```

This command tells `wasm-pack` to build our project and output the generated WebAssembly and JavaScript wrapper files in a `pkg` directory.

Setting Up JavaScript Integration

Now that we have our WebAssembly module, let's set up a simple JavaScript application to use it. Create a new directory called `web` inside the `wasm_example` directory. In this `web` directory, create an

`index.html` and a `index.js` file. ### index.html

Here is a basic `index.html` file to load our WebAssembly and JavaScript code:

```html
<!DOCTYPE html>
<html lang="en">
<head>
<meta charset="UTF-8">
<meta name="viewport" content="width=device-width, initial-scale=1.0">
<title>Rust + WebAssembly Example</title>
<script type="module" src="index.js"></script>
</head>
<body>
<h1>Rust + WebAssembly with JavaScript Integration</h1>
```

69

```html
<button id="addButton">Add Numbers</button>
<p id="result"></p>
</body>
</html>
```

index.js

Now, in `index.js`, we'll load our WebAssembly module and integrate it with the existing JavaScript code:

```javascript
import init, { add } from '../pkg/wasm_example.js';

async function run() {
// Initialize the WebAssembly module await init();


const button = document.getElementById('addButton');
const result = document.getElementById('result');
// Use the add function when the button is clicked
button.addEventListener('click', () => {

const sum = add(5, 7);

result.textContent = `The sum is: ${sum}`;

});
}
run();
```

Here, we import our `init` function from the generated

JavaScript file that was created during the build process, and we also import the `add` function we defined in Rust.

Running Your Application

To test the application, you need to serve it through a web server. You can use a simple HTTP server like

`http-server`, which you can install via npm:

```bash
npm install -g http-server
```

Now, navigate to the `web` directory and run:

```bash
http-server .
```

Open your browser and navigate to `http://localhost:8080` (or whatever port is specified). Click on the "Add Numbers" button, and you should see the result being displayed on the screen.

In this chapter, we explored the powerful combination of Rust and WebAssembly, leveraging Rust's performance and safety alongside JavaScript's flexibility and ecosystem. We walked through setting up the development environment, writing Rust code that can be compiled to WebAssembly, and finally integrating it with JavaScript in a web application.

Chapter 5: Working with Data in Rust for WebAssembly

The ability to work with data efficiently is pivotal for any application, especially web applications that need to interact with the browser's Document Object Model (DOM) and perform real-time updates. Rust's type system, memory safety, and performance make it an excellent candidate for developing high-performance applications in WASM. We will cover topics such as data types, managing memory, serialization and deserialization, and interacting with JavaScript.

5.1 Understanding Data Types in Rust

Rust offers a rich type system that allows developers to define data structures that fit their application needs. Basic data types in Rust include integers, floats, booleans, and characters, but when working with WebAssembly, we also want to leverage more complex types such as structs, enums, and collections.

5.1.1 Primitive Types Primitive types in Rust include:

- **Integers**: i8, i16, i32, i64, u8, u16, u32, u64

Floating-point numbers: f32, f64

Booleans: bool

Characters: char

When compiled to WebAssembly, these types are converted to their WASM equivalents, and understanding their sizes and representation is crucial while writing performance-sensitive code.

5.1.2 Complex Types #### Structs

Structs in Rust are user-defined data types that are used to create complex data structures. Here is an example of a simple struct representing a user profile:

```rust
struct UserProfile{ name: String, age: u32,
}
```

Enums

Enums allow you to define a type that can be one of many variants. This feature is very useful for creating flexible and expressive APIs:

```rust
enum Message { Text(String), Number(u32),
}
```

5.2 Memory Management in WebAssembly

WebAssembly has a linear memory model, meaning memory is represented as a contiguous array of bytes. Rust's ownership system provides a robust way of managing memory, reducing the chances of memory leaks and undefined behavior.

5.2.1 Allocation and Deallocation

Rust's standard library uses allocation and deallocation methods like `Box`, `Rc`, and `Arc` to handle memory. While in WebAssembly, it's essential to manage linear memory explicitly using the `wasm- bindgen` library or `wasm32-unknown-unknown` target.

To allocate and deallocate memory in Rust for WASM, you do this:

```rust
#[wasm_bindgen]
pub fn create_user_profile(name: String, age: u32) -> *mut UserProfile { let profile = Box::new(UserProfile { name, age }); Box::into_raw(profile)
}

#[wasm_bindgen]
pub fn free_user_profile(profile: *mut UserProfile) { if profile.is_null() { return; }

unsafe { Box::from_raw(profile); } // Deallocate memory
}
```

5.3 Serialization and Deserialization

For web applications to communicate effectively, they often need to serialize data into JSON or other formats that can be sent over the network. Rust has various libraries, such as `serde`, which is a powerful serialization framework.

5.3.1 Using Serde

To use Serde, first, add it to your `Cargo.toml`:

```toml
[dependencies]
serde = { version = "1.0", features = ["derive"] }
serde_json = "1.0"
```

You can then derive `Serialize` and `Deserialize` for your

structs:

```rust
use serde::{Serialize, Deserialize};

#[derive(Serialize, Deserialize)] struct UserProfile {
name: String,
age: u32,
}
```

Now you can easily convert your struct to JSON and vice versa:

```rust
let user = UserProfile { name: "Alice".to_string(), age: 30 }; let json = serde_json::to_string(&user).unwrap();

let user_from_json: UserProfile = serde_json::from_str(&json).unwrap();
```

5.4 Interacting with JavaScript

Interfacing Rust with JavaScript is what makes WebAssembly powerful in web applications. Using the `wasm-bindgen` library, Rust functions can easily be callable from JavaScript, and vice versa. ### 5.4.1 Exposing Rust Functions to JavaScript

To expose a Rust function to JavaScript, annotate it with `#[wasm_bindgen]`:

```rust #[wasm_bindgen]
```

```rust
pub fn greet(name: &str) {
web_sys::console::log_1(&format!("Hello, {}!",
name).into());
}
```

5.4.2 Handling JavaScript Types

When interacting with JavaScript, especially when accepting parameters, you need `wasm-bindgen` types:

```rust
#[wasm_bindgen]
pub fn take_array(arr: JsArray) { for value in arr.iter() {
let number = value.as_f64().unwrap();
web_sys::console::log_1(&format!("Received number: {}",
number).into());
}
}
```

We discussed the importance of Rust's type system, memory management, serialization, and how to interact with JavaScript code. With these foundational skills, you will be well-prepared to build efficient and safe web applications that harness the power of Rust and WebAssembly together.

Handling Strings, Arrays, and Complex Data Types in Rust

While its low-level capabilities make it an exceptional choice for system programming, it also offers a rich set of features for managing memory safely and effectively, particularly when dealing with strings, arrays, and more complex data types. In this chapter, we will explore how to efficiently handle these foundational elements in Rust, including ownership, borrowing, and the various types provided by the language.

1. Strings in Rust ### 1.1 The String Type

In Rust, strings come in two primary forms: `String` and string slices (`&str`).

`String` is an owned, growable string type, which is stored on the heap. It allows for dynamic memory allocation, making it suitable for cases where the string's content can change at runtime.

`&str` is a string slice, which is a reference to a portion of a string. This type is immutable and generally used for string literals or for borrowing a portion of a `String`.

1.2 Creating and Modifying Strings

Creating a new `String` can be done using the `String::new()` method, or by using the `to_string()` method on string literals.

```rust
fn main() {
let     mut     my_string     =     String::new();
```

```
my_string.push_str("Hello,  ");   my_string.push('W');
my_string.push_str("orld!"); println!("{}", my_string);
}
```
` ` `

In the above example, we demonstrate how to create a new string and modify it by using `push_str()` for adding strings and `push()` for adding single characters.

1.3 String Slices

To create a string slice, you can simply borrow a part of a `String`.

` ` `rust

```
fn main() {

let my_string = String::from("Hello, World!"); let
my_slice: &str = &my_string[0..5];  //  "Hello"
println!("{}", my_slice);

}
```
` ` `

In this example, we borrowed the first five characters of `my_string`. String slices allow you to efficiently reference string data without taking ownership.

1.4 Joining and Splitting Strings

Rust provides several methods for joining and splitting strings. The `join()` method is particularly useful with arrays of strings.

` ` `rust

```
fn main() {
```

```rust
let strings = vec!["Hello", "World"]; let sentence = strings.join(", ");
println!("{}", sentence); // "Hello, World"
}
```

For splitting strings, you can use the `split()` method, which creates an iterator over the substrings.

```rust
fn main() {
let string = String::from("one,two,three");
let parts: Vec<&str> = string.split(",").collect();
println!("{:?}", parts); // ["one", "two", "three"]
}
```

2. Arrays in Rust ### 2.1 The Array Type

Arrays in Rust are fixed-size sequences of elements of the same type. They are allocated on the stack and are defined with square brackets.

```rust
fn main() {
let numbers: [i32; 5] = [1, 2, 3, 4, 5];
println!("{:?}", numbers);
}
```

The type annotation `[i32; 5]` indicates an array of five

32-bit integers. ### 2.2 Accessing and Modifying Arrays

Accessing elements in an array is straightforward. You can use indexing to retrieve or modify elements.

```rust
fn main() {

let mut numbers = [1, 2, 3, 4, 5]; println!("{}", numbers[0]); // Output: 1 numbers[0] = 10;

println!("{:?}", numbers); // Output: [10, 2, 3, 4, 5]
}
```

2.3 Slices

Rust also supports slices which are a dynamically-sized view into a contiguous sequence of elements.

```rust
fn main() {

let numbers = [1, 2, 3, 4, 5];

let slice: &[i32] = &numbers[1..4]; // Slices from index 1 to 3 println!("{:?}", slice); // Output: [2, 3, 4]
}
```

Using slices allows for flexible manipulation of array data without needing to copy the data itself. ## 3. Complex Data Types

Rust allows for the creation of more complex data types using structs, enums, and tuples. These structures provide a way to bundle related data together.

80

3.1 Structs

Structs in Rust are used to create custom data types that can contain multiple fields.

```rust
struct Person { name: String, age: u32,
}
fn main() {
let person = Person {
name: String::from("Alice"), age: 30,
};
println!("Name: {}, Age: {}", person.name, person.age);
}
```

Here, `Person` is a struct that groups a name and an age. Instances of structs can be created and manipulated as needed.

3.2 Enums

Enums are a powerful feature of Rust, allowing the definition of a type that can be one of several specified variants.

```rust
enum Direction { North,
South, East, West,
}
```

```rust
fn main() {
let dir = Direction::North; match dir {
Direction::North => println!("Going North!"),
_ => println!("Going another direction"),
}
}
```

In this example, we defined an enum `Direction` and then used pattern matching to handle different cases. Rust's enums can also be combined with structs to create more complex types.

3.3 Tuples

Tuples are fixed-size collections that can contain multiple different types.

```rust
fn main() {
let tuple: (i32, f64, String) = (42, 3.14, String::from("Hello")); println!("Tuple values: {} {} {}", tuple.0, tuple.1, tuple.2);
}
```

Tuples are particularly useful for returning multiple values from a function.

The language's strong emphasis on ownership and borrowing ensures that memory is managed safely and efficiently. Understanding these fundamental data types not only lays the foundation for effective programming in Rust but also enhances your ability to create high-performance applications. As you continue your journey with Rust, mastering these concepts will empower you to build robust solutions for an array of problems.

Passing Data Between JavaScript and Rust: Interoperability Basics

JavaScript, with its non-blocking asynchronous capabilities and vast ecosystem, is a powerful language for web development. Conversely, Rust offers a robust framework for systems programming, with safety guarantees and performance akin to that of C and C++. This chapter explores the fundamentals of interoperability between JavaScript and Rust, providing insights into modern techniques that enable seamless communication between the two languages.

The Need for Interoperability

Understanding the need for interoperability between JavaScript and Rust is crucial. JavaScript excels in handling user interfaces, web APIs, and event-driven architecture, while Rust shines in tasks requiring heavy computation, memory safety, and concurrency. By leveraging the strengths of both languages, developers can build applications that are not only performant but also maintainable and safe.

Use Cases for Interoperability

WebAssembly (Wasm): Rust can be compiled to WebAssembly, enabling high-performance functions to be executed in the browser. This integration is particularly beneficial for computationally intensive tasks such as image processing, scientific simulations, and game development.

Node.js Add-ons: Rust can be used to create native add-ons for Node.js, enhancing server-side performance and allowing developers to write performance-critical code in Rust while maintaining the convenience of JavaScript for the rest of the application.

Browser Extensions: Interoperability is useful in developing browser extensions where performance, security, and efficiency are paramount.

Setting Up the Environment

Before diving into the interoperability basics, ensure you have the necessary tools installed:

Rust: Install Rust using `rustup`. This toolchain will allow you to manage different versions of Rust.

```bash
curl --proto '=https' --tlsv1.2 -sSf https://sh.rustup.rs | sh
```

Node.js: Download and install Node.js from the official website, ensuring you have the latest version.

wasm-pack: This tool aids in building and packaging Rust-generated WebAssembly. You can install it with:

```bash
cargo install wasm-pack
```

Compiling Rust to WebAssembly

To pass data effectively, we must first understand how to compile Rust into WebAssembly. Here is a simple example that highlights creating a Rust function and invoking it from JavaScript.

Create a New Rust Project:

```bash
cargo new wasm_project --lib cd wasm_project
```

Configure `Cargo.toml`:

Add the following dependencies to your `Cargo.toml` file to enable WebAssembly integration:

```toml
[lib]
crate-type = ["cdylib"]
[dependencies]
wasm-bindgen = "0.2"
```

Write Rust Code:

Edit `src/lib.rs` to include a simple function that manipulates data:

```rust
use wasm_bindgen::prelude::*;
#[wasm_bindgen]
pub fn add(a: i32, b: i32) -> i32 { a + b
}
```

```

```

Build the Project:

Run the following command to compile the Rust code to WebAssembly:

```bash
wasm-pack build --target web
```

This will create a `pkg` directory containing the compiled WebAssembly module and JavaScript bindings. ## Integrating with JavaScript

Now that we have our Rust code compiled to WebAssembly, we can integrate it with JavaScript. Let's create a simple HTML file to interact with our Rust-generated Wasm module:

Setup HTML file:

Create an `index.html` file in the same directory:

```html
<!DOCTYPE html>
<html lang="en">
<head>
<meta charset="UTF-8">
<meta name="viewport" content="width=device-width, initial-scale=1.0">
<title>Wasm with Rust and JavaScript</title>
<script type="module">
```

```
import init, { add } from './pkg/wasm_project.js';
async function run() { await init();
const result = add(5, 3); console.log("5 + 3 = ", result);
}
run();
</script>
</head>
<body>
<h1>Wasm with Rust and JavaScript</h1>
</body>
</html>
```

Serve the Application:

You can use a simple server, like `http-server`, to serve the application. Install it via npm and run:

```bash
npm install -g http-server http-server .
```

Navigate to `http://localhost:8080` in your browser to see the results. ## Passing Complex Data Structures

Real applications require more than simple integers; you may want to pass complex data structures like arrays or objects. Using `wasm-bindgen`, you can easily handle these data types:

Passing Arrays

Rust allows you to pass slices (essentially arrays) from JavaScript. Here's how to modify our Rust code:

Modify Rust Code:

Update your `src/lib.rs` to add a function that accepts an array:

```rust
#[wasm_bindgen]
pub fn sum_array(arr: &[i32]) -> i32 { arr.iter().sum()
}
```

Update JavaScript Code:

Modify your JavaScript to call this function:

```javascript
const array = [1, 2, 3, 4, 5]; const sum = sum_array(array);
console.log("Sum of array: ", sum);
```

Recompile and Serve:

Recompile your Rust code and start your server again to see the changes reflected in your application.

This chapter laid the groundwork for passing data between the two languages, highlighting key concepts and practical examples, which serve as a foundation for further exploration of Rust's capabilities within JavaScript environments. As you delve deeper into interoperability, consider exploring more complex data types, error handling, and advanced use cases that can harness the full potential of both languages.

Chapter 6: Error Handling and Debugging in Rust WebAssembly Projects

In this chapter, we will explore the nuances of error handling in Rust, strategies for debugging your Wasm applications, and tools that can enhance your debugging experience.

6.1 Understanding Error Handling in Rust

Error handling in Rust is designed to be explicit and intentional, promoting clarity and reliability. Rust provides two primary types for handling errors: `Result` and `Option`.

6.1.1 The `Result` Type

The `Result` type is used for functions that can return an error. It is an enumeration that can be either

`Ok(T)` for successful results or `Err(E)` for errors:

```rust
fn divide(a: f64, b: f64) -> Result<f64, String> { if b == 0.0 {
Err("Division by zero".to_string())
} else {
Ok(a / b)
}
}
```

In this example, the `divide` function returns a `Result` type. If the division is successful, it returns the quotient wrapped in `Ok`; otherwise, it returns an error message wrapped in `Err`.

6.1.2 The `Option` Type

The `Option` type is used when there may or may not be a value. It represents either `Some(T)` for a value or `None` when there is no value:

```rust
fn find_index(vec: &[i32], value: i32) -> Option<usize> {
    vec.iter().position(|&x| x == value)
}
```

The `find_index` function returns `Some(index)` if the value is found and `None` if it is not. ### 6.1.3 Handling Errors Gracefully

When working with WebAssembly, it's essential to handle errors gracefully, especially when returning results to JavaScript. Use the `wasm_bindgen` crate to convert Rust errors into JavaScript-friendly formats:

```rust
use wasm_bindgen::prelude::*;

#[wasm_bindgen]
pub fn safe_divide(a: f64, b: f64) -> Result<f64, JsValue> { divide(a, b).map_err(|err| JsValue::from_str(&err))
}
```

90

Here, the `safe_divide` function converts Rust errors into JavaScript values, allowing for rich error handling on the frontend.

6.2 Common Error Patterns in WebAssembly

When developing web applications using Rust and WebAssembly, you might encounter specific error patterns:

6.2.1 Runtime Errors

Runtime errors occur due to unexpected behaviors in the browser. These can be handled using a combination of `panic` hooks and `Result` types.

```rust #[wasm_bindgen]

pub fn risky_operation() -> Result<(), JsValue> { let result = some_fallible_function()?; Ok(result)

}
```

6.2.2 Integration Errors

When Rust interacts with JavaScript, integration errors can arise—such as mismatched arguments or unexpected types. To mitigate these issues, use type-checks and ensure proper conversions between Rust and JavaScript types.

```rust #[wasm_bindgen]

pub fn process_array(arr: &JsValue) -> Result<Vec<i32>, JsValue> {

let array: Vec<i32> = arr.into_serde().map_err(|e| JsValue::from_str(&e.to_string()))?; Ok(array)
```

```
}
```
```

## 6.3 Debugging Techniques for Rust WebAssembly

Debugging Rust code compiled to WebAssembly can be challenging. However, various techniques and tools can help ease this process.

### 6.3.1 Logging

Use the `console_log` crate to log messages to the JavaScript console. Set up a logger at the beginning of your application:

```rust

use console_log;

fn main() {

console_log::init_with_level(log::Level::Debug).expect("error initializing logger"); log::info!("Application started");

}
```
```

6.3.2 Debugging with Source Maps

By enabling debugging information when compiling your Rust code to Wasm, you can generate source maps that map the compiled code back to the original Rust source. This allows for easier debugging in browsers' dev tools.

```bash

wasm-pack build --dev --target web
```
```

### 6.3.3 Browser Developer Tools
```

Modern browsers offer extensive developer tools that support debugging WebAssembly. You can set breakpoints, inspect memory, and evaluate expressions directly in the browser.

6.3.4 Using `wasm-bindgen` and `wasm-pack`

Utilize `wasm-bindgen` for generating bindings that allow you to interact seamlessly with JavaScript. This enhances your debugging experience as you can trace issues directly back to the respective JS calls.

6.4 Best Practices for Error Handling and Debugging

Leverage `Result` and `Option`: Always prefer explicit error handling using `Result` and `Option`.

Convert errors gracefully: Use `JsValue` to handle errors across Rust and JavaScript seamlessly.

Utilize dev tools: Familiarize yourself with browser developer tools for effective debugging.

Maintain comprehensive logging: Implement logging across your application to capture errors and important events.

Write tests: Use unit tests and integration tests to catch potential errors early in the development cycle.

By understanding the error types provided by Rust, using effective debugging techniques, and employing best practices, you can create resilient applications that handle unexpected conditions and run smoothly in the web environment. As you continue your journey with Rust and WebAssembly, these skills will be invaluable in ensuring your application's success.

Managing Errors in Rust: Results, Options, and Panic Handling

This chapter will explore Rust's error handling mechanisms, focusing on the `Result` and `Option` types, as well as the concept of panicking when facing unrecoverable conditions.

1. Understanding Errors in Rust

Rust categorizes errors into two main types: recoverable and unrecoverable errors. Recoverable errors are those that a program can handle gracefully, typically through the use of types like `Result`. Unrecoverable errors, on the other hand, often indicate a serious problem with the program logic or environment that would make further execution unsafe or meaningless; for these situations, Rust utilizes panics.

1.1. Recoverable Errors

Recoverable errors arise in situations where a program can proceed with alternative logic or user input. For instance, if a program attempts to read from a file that does not exist, it is possible to either create the file, prompt the user for a different file path, or log an error for further investigation. In Rust, the `Result` type encapsulates these scenarios.

1.1.1. The Result Type The `Result` enum is defined as:

```rust
enum Result<T, E> {

Ok(T),// Represents a successful outcome with associated data of type T Err(E), // Represents a failure with
```

associated error of type E

}

```
```

The `Result` type takes two type parameters: `T` for the successful value and `E` for the error value. This design allows developers to implement custom error types, promoting better abstractions and clearer error handling.

Example of Using Result:

```rust
use std::fs::File;

use std::io::{self, Read};

fn read_file(file_path: &str) -> Result<String, io::Error> {
let mut file = File::open(file_path)?;

let mut contents = String::new();
file.read_to_string(&mut contents)?; Ok(contents)

}

fn main() {

match read_file("my_file.txt") {

Ok(data) => println!("File contents: {}", data), Err(e) => println!("Error reading file: {}", e),


}

}
```

In the above example, file reading operations can fail; for

instance, the file may not exist. Using the `?` operator helps propagate errors seamlessly with `Result`.

1.2. Unrecoverable Errors

Unrecoverable errors signify flaws in the logic of the program, such as division by zero or an out-of-bounds array index. For these cases, Rust encourages developers to use the `panic!` macro.

1.2.1. Panic Handling

When a `panic!` occurs, the program will stop execution, unwinding the stack as it goes. This means any resources held by the program will be cleaned up. Panic should be used sparingly and primarily for situations that should not occur during normal operation.

Example of Panic:

```rust
fn divide(num: i32, denom: i32) -> i32 { if denom == 0 {
panic!("Attempted to divide by zero!");
}
num / denom
}
```

In this case, should `denom` be zero, calling the `divide` function will trigger a panic, leading to an immediate halt in program execution.

2. The Option Type

While the `Result` type captures situations involving

potential errors with recoverable outcomes, sometimes it is necessary to represent a value that may be absent. The `Option` enum serves this purpose.

2.1. The Option Type Definition The `Option` enum is defined as:

```rust
enum Option<T> {

Some(T), // Represents a value of type T None,      // Represents the absence of a value

}
```

`Option` helps in scenarios where a function may legitimately return nothing, which reduces chances of null pointer dereferencing—a common source of bugs in many programming languages.

Example of Using Option:

```rust
fn find_item(list: &[i32], target: i32) -> Option<usize> {


for (index, &item) in list.iter().enumerate() { if item == target {

return Some(index);

}
}
None

}
```

97

```
fn main() {

let numbers = vec![1, 2, 3, 4, 5]; match
find_item(&numbers, 3) {

Some(index) => println!("Item found at index: {}", index),
None => println!("Item not found."),

}

}
```
` ` `

This example illustrates how an absence of a value is clearly conveyed through the `Option` type, allowing for safe handling of potentially missing data.

3. Combining Result and Option

In practice, Rust developers may often find themselves using `Result` and `Option` together to model complex error handling scenarios. For example, a function might return `Option<Result<T, E>>` when the success condition is uncertain, requiring both absence handling and error handling.

By differentiating between recoverable and unrecoverable errors and providing robust constructs to manage these cases, Rust sets a high standard for reliability in programming. Understanding and leveraging these patterns is essential for any Rust programmer aiming to create efficient and robust applications.

Debugging Rust and WebAssembly with DevTools and Logging Techniques

The integration of Rust and WebAssembly brings tremendous advantages but also introduces new challenges, primarily around debugging. This chapter explores how to efficiently debug Rust and WebAssembly applications using browser DevTools, effective logging techniques, and best practices to streamline the debugging process.

Understanding WebAssembly Debugging

Debugging WebAssembly applications differs significantly from debugging traditional web applications. Wasm binaries are low-level code streams that make direct inspection difficult. However, with the right tools and techniques, developers can gain insight into the execution flow and quickly identify issues.

1. Compiling for Debugging

The first step in debugging a Rust and WebAssembly application is ensuring that the code is compiled with debugging information. The Rust compiler allows developers to compile with additional flags to include source maps, which are necessary for debugging:

```bash
wasm-pack build --dev
```

By using the `--dev` flag, you instruct `wasm-pack` to compile the code in development mode. This setting produces a smaller WebAssembly file and generates source maps that map to your original Rust codebase.

2. Setting Up the Environment

To effectively debug Wasm code running in the browser, setting up the right environment is critical. The modern web browsers, including Google Chrome and Mozilla Firefox, provide robust DevTools for this purpose. To inspect, debug, and profile your Rust and WebAssembly applications, follow these steps:

Include Source Maps: Ensure that source maps are included when packaging your application, as mentioned earlier. This will allow browser DevTools to map your Rust code to the corresponding WebAssembly code.

Serve via a Web Server: Use a local web server to serve your application rather than opening the file directly in a browser, as this may lead to cross-origin issues that affect debugging.

Open DevTools: Launch the DevTools in your browser, typically using F12 or right-clicking on the page and selecting "Inspect." Navigate to the "Sources" tab, where you can see the loaded Wasm modules.

3. Using DevTools for Debugging

Once the environment is set up, you can utilize the features in DevTools to inspect and debug your Rust and WebAssembly code.

Breakpoints: You can set breakpoints in your Rust code directly from the DevTools interface. This allows you to pause execution and inspect variable values, call stacks, and control flow, just like you would in JavaScript debugging.

Step Through Code: Use the stepping features (`Step Over`, `Step Into`, and `Step Out`) to navigate through your Rust functions and track down issues in logic or execution paths.

Variable Inspection: Inspect local and global variables in the scope of where the breakpoint was hit. This helps identify any unexpected values or states in your application.

Console Logging: Utilize the console to log output from your Rust application. This is essential for verifying the flow of execution and for checking variable states.

4. Logging Techniques

Effective logging is an indispensable tool for any debugging process. In Rust, developers can use the `log` crate, which provides a flexible logging framework. To implement logging in your Rust and WebAssembly application, follow these steps:

Add Dependencies: In your `Cargo.toml`, add the necessary dependencies:

```toml
[dependencies] log = "0.4"

wasm-bindgen = "0.2"
```

Set Up a Logger: Use a compatible logger implementation, such as `console_log`, to direct Rust logs to the JavaScript console:

```rust
use wasm_bindgen::prelude::*; use log::{info, error};

#[wasm_bindgen(start)] pub fn main() {

console_log::init_with_level(log::Level::Debug).expect("e
```

rror initializing logger"); info!("Application started");

error!("An error occurred");

```
}
```
` ` `

Log Important Events: Throughout your code, use different log levels (`error!`, `warn!`, `info!`,

`debug!`, and `trace!`) strategically. This helps monitor the health of your application and identify the points of failure.

Inspect Logs in DevTools: Open the console in DevTools to view the logs created by your Rust application. This provides real-time feedback while the application runs.

5. Common Issues and Solutions

Debugging Rust and WebAssembly may introduce specific challenges. Here are a few common issues and their solutions:

Error Handling: Rust emphasizes strict error handling. Ensure that you properly address errors using Rust's `Result` and `Option` types to avoid unexpected panics when translating this behavior to WebAssembly.

Data Types and Memory Management: WebAssembly has limitations on how it handles memory. Be cognizant of Rust's ownership and borrowing concepts, particularly when sharing data between Rust and JavaScript.

Performance Bottlenecks: Use the performance profiling tools in DevTools to identify potential bottlenecks in your application. Look for functions that take longer to execute and consider optimizing them.

By compiling for debugging, leveraging browser DevTools, and implementing robust logging practices, you're equipped to trace and resolve issues within your application efficiently. Each debugging session is a learning opportunity, paving the way for better coding practices and more resilient applications. Embrace the challenge, and allow your creativity to flow free, knowing that effective debugging is at your fingertips!

Chapter 7: Performance Optimization with Rust and WebAssembly

The combination of Rust and WebAssembly (often abbreviated as wasm) presents a powerful solution to not only meet these demands but exceed them. This chapter delves into how Rust, with its emphasis on safety, concurrency, and performance, can be utilized alongside WebAssembly to create high-performance applications running in web browsers.

7.1 Understanding WebAssembly

Before diving into the optimization techniques, it is essential to comprehend what WebAssembly is. WebAssembly is a low-level binary format that allows code written in languages such as C, C++, and Rust to run on the web. It is designed to provide a portable compilation target for high-level languages, enabling developers to run high-performance applications in web browsers at near-native speeds. The primary advantages of WebAssembly include:

Performance: It allows code to run faster in browser environments compared to JavaScript.

Security: WebAssembly is executed in a safe, sandboxed execution environment, minimizing vector attack risks.

Portability: Code can be compiled to WebAssembly and executed on different platforms without modification.

Interoperability: It can work alongside JavaScript, allowing developers to leverage existing codebases while optimizing performance-critical sections with Rust.

7.2 Why Rust?

Rust has gained popularity not just for system programming but also for web development due to its distinctive features:

Memory Safety: Rust's ownership model guarantees memory safety without a garbage collector, which means fewer runtime errors and predictable performance.

Zero-Cost Abstractions: Rust's abstractions, such as iterators and closures, do not impose additional overhead, making it suitable for performance-sensitive applications.

Concurrency: Rust equips developers with tools to write concurrent code safely, resulting in applications that can perform multiple tasks simultaneously without compromising performance.

Combining Rust with WebAssembly allows developers to write high-performance code that can easily be deployed on the web.

7.3 Setting Up the Development Environment

To begin optimizing performance with Rust and WebAssembly, developers must set up their environment. Here's a quick guide:

Install Rust: Ensure that Rust is installed. You can do this by downloading it from [Rust's official website](https://www.rust-lang.org/).

```bash
curl --proto '=https' --tlsv1.2 -sSf https://sh.rustup.rs | sh
```

Install the WebAssembly Target:

```bash
rustup target add wasm32-unknown-unknown
```

Set Up the Required Tools:
Use `cargo` to create a new Rust project:

```bash
cargo new my_wasm_project --lib cd my_wasm_project
```

Install `wasm-pack`: This tool simplifies building and packaging Rust-generated WebAssembly. Install it using:

```bash
cargo install wasm-pack
```

With the environment ready, developers can proceed to create and build their Rust applications that target WebAssembly.

7.4 Building a Simple WebAssembly Module

Let's create a simple example to illustrate how Rust can be used to optimize performance. Below is a Rust function that computes the Fibonacci sequence, which is a classic example often used to demonstrate performance optimizations.

In `src/lib.rs`, you might write:

```rust
#[no_mangle]
pub extern "C" fn fibonacci(n: u32) -> u32 { if n <= 1 {
return n;
}
fibonacci(n - 1) + fibonacci(n - 2)
}
```

This function computes Fibonacci numbers recursively. Although the recursive implementation is not optimal, it serves to illustrate the integration with WebAssembly. With `wasm-pack`, compile the Rust code to WebAssembly:

```bash
wasm-pack build --target web
```

Once compiled, JavaScript can easily invoke the `fibonacci` function exported by the WebAssembly module. ## 7.5 Performance Optimization Techniques Now that we have our basic WebAssembly module, we can explore various techniques to optimize performance further.

7.5.1 Use of Efficient Algorithms

While constructing applications that require complex computations, selecting the right algorithm is essential.

For instance, the naive Fibonacci implementation can be replaced with an iterative or memoized version to drastically improve performance.

7.5.2 Reduce Memory Allocations

Memory management is crucial. Rust's ownership model ensures that memory is allocated efficiently. Minimizing allocations, reusing buffers, and avoiding unnecessary copies will lead to performance boosts.

7.5.3 Leverage SIMD (Single Instruction, Multiple Data)

Recent advancements in WebAssembly allow for SIMD operations, enabling data parallelism which can significantly speed up computations. Utilizing SIMD can enhance performance for applications like image processing or numerical computations.

7.5.4 Minimize Interoperability Overhead

Every time JavaScript interacts with WebAssembly, there is some overhead. To minimize this, batch multiple calls together or keep processing within WebAssembly where possible, reducing back-and-forth communication.

7.5.5 Optimize Compilation Settings

By tweaking the compilation settings, developers can achieve better performance. For example, compiling with optimizations enabled:

```bash
wasm-pack build --release
```

7.6 Real-World Applications of Rust and WebAssembly

The optimizations discussed apply to several practical applications:

Game Development: Many game developers use Rust and WebAssembly for creating high- performance game engines.

Data Visualization: Libraries built with Rust can be compiled to WebAssembly for efficient rendering of complex visualizations.

Cryptography: Secure and efficient cryptographic algorithms can greatly benefit from Rust's performance when compiled to WebAssembly.

By leveraging Rust's safety and concurrency features alongside WebAssembly's execution efficiency, developers can craft high-performance applications capable of delivering seamless user experiences. As web technology continues to evolve, the combination of Rust and WebAssembly is poised to play a crucial role in shaping the future of web development.

Profiling and Benchmarking WebAssembly Code for Faster Execution

One of the primary advantages of using Rust for WebAssembly development is its focus on memory safety and zero-cost abstractions, which can translate to significant performance benefits. However, to fully exploit these advantages, developers must engage in profiling and benchmarking their WebAssembly code. This chapter delves into strategies to optimize performance through systematic profiling and benchmarking, with an emphasis on Rust programming.

Understanding WebAssembly

Before we dive into profiling and benchmarking, it's essential to understand what WebAssembly is and how it differs from traditional web technologies. WebAssembly is a binary instruction format designed to be a portable compilation target for high-level languages. It executes in a safe, fast, and efficient manner, comparable to native machine code.

For Rust developers, compiling to WebAssembly is straightforward, thanks to tools like `wasm-pack` and

`rustup`. However, ensuring the efficiency of the resulting code requires diligent attention to various performance metrics.

Profiling: Identify Bottlenecks

Profiling is the process of measuring the space (memory) or time complexity of an algorithm while it is executing. In the context of WebAssembly, profiling helps identify bottlenecks that hinder performance.

Tools for Profiling Rust WebAssembly

Chrome DevTools: A powerful tool for profiling WebAssembly executed in a browser. The Performance tab can be used to analyze the performance of WebAssembly modules in the same way as regular JavaScript.

WasmFiddle: An online editor that allows for testing WebAssembly applications. Though it focuses on simplicity, it lacks refined profiling tools; however, it's still useful for rapid prototyping.

wasm-opt: This tool optimizes WebAssembly binaries

and provides potential insights into performance improvements. It allows you to check the size of the output binary and offers various optimization levels.

Instrumentation Libraries: Libraries like `flamegraph` and `perf` can be used to generate flame graphs to visualize where your application spends most of its execution time.

Steps to Profile Rust WebAssembly Code

Compile with Debug Information: Start by compiling your Rust code with debug information enabled. This will allow the profiler to provide more detailed insights.

```bash
wasm-pack build --debug
```

Run the Application: Deploy your application in a local server environment and access it through a browser.

Collect Profiling Data: Use Chrome DevTools to record performance while the application runs.

Analyze the Results: Review the collected data to identify functions or operations that consume excessive resources.

Benchmarking: Assessing Performance

Once bottlenecks are identified through profiling, benchmarking provides a way to evaluate how changes to your code affect its performance. Benchmarking is critical for validating performance optimizations and ensuring that they yield the expected improvements.

Setting Up a Benchmarking Environment

Use `criterion.rs`: This is a powerful and flexible benchmarking library for Rust. It provides detailed statistical information about the performance of your functions.

Create Benchmark Tests: Set up `Criterion` benchmarks in a separate module within your project. Define benchmarks for critical functions that are likely performance-sensitive.

```rust
#[macro_use]
extern crate criterion; use criterion::Criterion;

fn benchmark_function() {
// your performance-sensitive code here
}

fn benchmark(c: &mut Criterion) {
c.bench_function("critical_function",    |b|    b.iter(||
benchmark_function()));
}

criterion_group!(benches,                          benchmark);
criterion_main!(benches);
```

Run Benchmarks: Execute the benchmarks and analyze the results. ### Tips for Effective Benchmarking

Isolate Benchmarks: Ensure that benchmarks run independently to avoid interference from other processes.

Multiple Runs: Execute benchmarks multiple times to obtain accurate results. `Criterion` handles this automatically.

Profile During Benchmarking: Use profiling tools like those mentioned above simultaneously to correlate performance metrics with the actual execution of your benchmarks.

Optimization Strategies

After gathering insights from profiling and benchmarking, you can begin to optimize your WebAssembly code. Here are some strategies specific to Rust and WebAssembly:

1. Optimize Data Structures

Choose data structures that offer efficient access and manipulation. Rust's collections provide various trade-offs; select the one that benefits your use case most.

2. Minimize Memory Allocations

Frequent memory allocations can lead to performance degradation. Use Rust's ownership model and lifetimes efficiently to manage memory allocations and deallocations.

3. Use Intrinsics and Unsafe Code

In cases where utmost performance is required, consider using Rust's `unsafe` code features or intrinsic functions. While this requires a solid understanding, it can yield considerable performance improvements when done correctly.

4. Enable Compiler Optimizations

When compiling your code for release, ensure you enable compiler optimizations:

```bash
```

```
wasm-pack build --release
```
```
```

By implementing these practices, developers can identify performance bottlenecks, validate optimizations, and ultimately deliver faster, more responsive web applications. As the Rust ecosystem for WebAssembly continues to grow, mastering these techniques will enable developers to harness the full potential of WebAssembly, providing an optimal experience for users across the web.

Leveraging Rust Features for High-Performance Applications

This chapter explores how various features of Rust can be harnessed to create applications that push the limits of performance, while maintaining a focus on safety and concurrency.

Memory Safety and Zero-Cost Abstractions

One of Rust's standout features is its approach to memory management. Unlike languages that rely on garbage collection, Rust uses a system of ownership with rules that the compiler checks at compile time. This results in zero-cost abstractions, enabling developers to write high-level code without suffering the performance penalties typically associated with such abstractions.

Ownership and Borrowing

At the core of Rust's memory safety is the ownership model, which eliminates data races and ensures that memory is managed predictably. This makes Rust an excellent choice for applications where performance is critical, such as game engines or real-time systems.

Ownership: Each value in Rust has a single owner, which dictates when the value is freed. This ownership model allows for fine-grained control over resource management without the need for manual memory handling, often leading to fewer bugs and crashes.

Borrowing: Rust allows references to values to be created through borrowing. Here, developers can either borrow immutably (shared references) or mutably (exclusive references), providing flexibility while ensuring safety.

By leveraging ownership and borrowing, developers can build systems that are both efficient and safe, with fewer opportunities for memory leaks and buffer overflows.

Performance Optimization Techniques

Rust provides a wealth of performance optimization opportunities that can be utilized to create efficient applications. These include features such as inline assembly, low-level hardware access, and efficient data structures.

Efficient Data Structures

Rust's standard library offers a variety of performant data structures that can be employed to maximize efficiency. For instance:

Vectors (`Vec<T>`) provide a contiguous growable array with optimized reallocation strategies.

Hash Maps (`HashMap<K, V>`) offer average-case constant-time complexity for insertions and lookups, essential for applications requiring quick access to large datasets.

Slices allow for safe, flexible access to collections of data without needing to copy or allocate new memory.

Utilizing these structures appropriately can streamline algorithms and minimize computational overhead. ### SIMD and Parallelism For applications requiring heavy computation, Rust's support for SIMD (Single Instruction, Multiple Data) allows developers to leverage modern CPUs effectively. By using crates like `packed_simd`, Rust can help you write code that performs operations across multiple data points in a single instruction cycle.

Additionally, Rust's built-in concurrency features facilitate the development of applications that can perform multiple tasks simultaneously. The `std::thread` module allows for easy thread creation, while the

`async`/`await` syntax simplifies asynchronous programming, making it easier to build I/O-bound applications, such as web servers or real-time data processing systems.

Profiling and Benchmarking

To truly optimize performance, developers should employ profiling and benchmarking tools. Rust provides built-in support for profiling through crates like `criterion` and `flamegraph`, enabling developers to analyze the performance of their code and identify bottlenecks.

By combining these tools with Rust's inherent safety features, developers can iteratively improve performance while ensuring that code remains free of concurrency issues and memory pitfalls.

116

Interfacing with Other Languages

For high-performance applications often embedded within larger systems, Rust provides excellent interoperability with languages like C and C++. This allows developers to write performance-critical components in Rust while leveraging existing C/C++ libraries.

Foreign Function Interface (FFI)

Rust's Foreign Function Interface (FFI) makes it straightforward to call C functions from Rust, providing direct access to low-level systems programming resources. This is particularly useful for developers needing to integrate with established codebases or require specific libraries that don't have a native Rust implementation.

Building Safe Interfaces

When interfacing with other languages, maintaining safety is paramount. Rust's safety guarantees can be maintained by creating wrappers that encapsulate the unsafe code, ensuring that any potential memory safety issues are mitigated. This allows developers to harness the speed of C/C++ while retaining the benefits of Rust's safety features.

Rust's unique combination of memory safety, performance, and concurrency makes it an exceptional choice for building high-performance applications. By leveraging Rust's ownership model, efficient data structures, parallelism, and FFI capabilities, developers can create robust systems that deliver outstanding performance while minimizing the risk of bugs and inefficiencies.

As the landscape of programming continues to evolve, Rust stands poised as a compelling alternative for developers seeking to balance high performance with the stringent safety and reliability requirements demanded by modern software applications. In a world where both speed and safety are paramount, Rust provides the tools and features necessary to succeed.

Chapter 8: Advanced Integration with JavaScript and WebAssembly

This chapter explores advanced integration techniques between Rust, JavaScript, and WebAssembly, providing you with the tools and knowledge to create highly interactive, efficient web applications.

1. Understanding WebAssembly and Its Role

Before diving into integration, it's crucial to understand what WebAssembly is. WebAssembly is a binary instruction format for a stack-based virtual machine that allows code written in high-level languages to run in the browser at near-native speed. WebAssembly is designed to complement JavaScript, enabling developers to build performance-sensitive sections of applications in a systems programming language like Rust.

1.1 Benefits of Using WebAssembly

Performance: WebAssembly executes at nearly native speed, making it suitable for computation-intensive tasks.

Portability: Wasm modules can run on any platform that supports a web browser, promoting code reuse.

Language Support: Beyond Rust, WebAssembly can be compiled from languages like C, C++, and Go, expanding your development toolkit.

2. Setting Up Your Rust Environment for WebAssembly

Before you can integrate Rust with JavaScript via WebAssembly, you need to set up your development environment correctly.

2.1 Installing Rust

Ensure you have Rust installed. If you haven't installed Rust yet, use the following command:

```bash
rustup install stable
```

2.2 Installing wasm-pack

`wasm-pack` is a CLI tool that makes it easy to build and package Rust-generated WebAssembly. Install it with:

```bash
cargo install wasm-pack
```

2.3 Setting Up a Rust Project for WebAssembly
Create a new Rust library project with:

```bash
cargo new --lib wasm_project cd wasm_project
```

2.4 Configuring `Cargo.toml`

Modify the `Cargo.toml` to include the necessary dependencies and to set the crate type to `cdylib`, which is essential for WebAssembly:

```toml
[package]
name = "wasm_project" version = "0.1.0"
edition = "2021"
```

```
[lib]
crate-type = ["cdylib"]
[dependencies]
wasm-bindgen = "0.2"
```

3. Writing Rust Code for WebAssembly

Let's write a simple Rust function that we will call from JavaScript. ### 3.1 Creating a Simple Function

Edit the `src/lib.rs` file and add a function that adds two numbers:

```rust
use wasm_bindgen::prelude::*;

#[wasm_bindgen]
pub fn add(a: i32, b: i32) -> i32 { a + b
}
```

3.2 Compiling to WebAssembly

Compile your project to WebAssembly using `wasm-pack`:

```bash
wasm-pack build --target web
```

This command generates a `pkg` directory containing your compiled Wasm binary and a JavaScript wrapper. ## 4. Integrating with JavaScript

Now that you have your Rust code compiled to WebAssembly, it's time to integrate it with a JavaScript frontend.

4.1 Setting Up HTML and JavaScript

Create an `index.html` file in the root of your project:

```html
<!DOCTYPE html>
<html lang="en">
<head>
<meta charset="UTF-8">
<meta name="viewport" content="width=device-width, initial-scale=1.0">
<title>Rust + WebAssembly</title>
<script type="module">
import init, { add } from './pkg/wasm_project.js';
async function run() {
await init(); // Initialize the wasm module
console.log(add(5, 7)); // Should print 12
}
run();
</script>
</head>
<body>
```

```
<h1>Rust WebAssembly Integration</h1>
</body>
</html>
```

4.2 Running Your Application

You can serve your HTML file using a simple HTTP server. If you have Python installed, run:

```bash
python -m http.server 8000
```

Open your browser and navigate to `http://localhost:8000` to see your application in action. Open the developer console to see the result of the addition operation.

5. Advanced Features and Best Practices

With basic integration complete, you may want to explore more advanced features and practices, such as: ### 5.1 Working with Complex Data Types

Rust and JavaScript can share complex data types, including arrays and objects. You can use `wasm-bindgen` to interface between Rust types and JavaScript.

5.2 Error Handling Across Languages

Learn how to handle errors in Rust and propagate them to JavaScript by using `Result` and `Option` types. ### 5.3 Seamless Interactivity Utilize `wasm-bindgen` features to create interactive web applications that respond to user actions. Explore the integration of Rust with web frameworks like Yew for sophisticated UI development.

5.4 Performance Optimization

Consider performance best practices such as minimizing the size of your Wasm binaries and optimizing for speed. Profiling tools can help identify bottlenecks in your code.

Integrating Rust with JavaScript and WebAssembly opens up a world of possibilities for developing high-performance web applications. As you become more comfortable with these technologies, you'll be able to leverage the strengths of each to create user experiences that are both rich and responsive. Continue exploring advanced features, optimizations, and best practices to ensure your applications remain at the forefront of web technology.

Using wasm-bindgen for Seamless JavaScript Interoperability

One of the most powerful tools for achieving this is `wasm-bindgen`, a Rust library that simplifies the process of binding Rust code to JavaScript. This chapter explores how to use `wasm-bindgen` to create smooth interoperability between Rust and JavaScript, allowing developers to harness the strengths of both languages in their web applications.

What is wasm-bindgen?

`wasm-bindgen` is a Rust library that facilitates communication between Rust and JavaScript during WebAssembly operations. It allows Rust code to be called from JavaScript and vice versa, enabling developers to write parts of their application in Rust while maintaining the ability to use JavaScript libraries, APIs, and frameworks.

With `wasm-bindgen`, you can:

Create Rust functions that are callable from JavaScript.

Interact with JavaScript objects and functions from Rust.

Pass data between Rust and JavaScript efficiently.

This creates a powerful platform for building complex web applications where performance is critical. ## Setting Up Your Rust Environment

Before diving into `wasm-bindgen`, ensure you have a proper Rust development environment set up. This includes:

Rust Installation: Make sure you have Rust installed. You can download and install Rust using [rustup](https://rustup.rs/), which is the recommended way to install Rust.

WebAssembly Toolchain: You will need to install the WebAssembly target. Use the following command:

```bash
rustup target add wasm32-unknown-unknown
```

npm and Node.js: Ensure you have Node.js and npm installed, as we will need them to manage JavaScript dependencies.

Installing wasm-bindgen CLI: You can install the `wasm-bindgen` command-line interface with:

```bash
cargo install wasm-bindgen-cli
```

Creating a New Project: Start a new Rust project using Cargo:

```bash
cargo new --lib wasm_interop_example cd wasm_interop_example
```

Add Dependencies: Update `Cargo.toml` to include `wasm-bindgen` as a dependency:

```toml
[dependencies]
wasm-bindgen = "0.2"
```

Writing Rust Code for JavaScript Interoperability

With your environment set up, let's create a simple Rust function that can be accessed from JavaScript. ### Example: A Simple Addition Function

Open the `src/lib.rs` file and write the following Rust code:

```rust
use wasm_bindgen::prelude::*;

#[wasm_bindgen]
pub fn add(a: i32, b: i32) -> i32 { a + b
```

```
}
```

In this example, we define a simple function `add` that takes two integers and returns their sum. The `#[wasm_bindgen]` attribute is crucial—it tells the compiler to expose this function to JavaScript. ### Building the Project

Next, compile the Rust code into WebAssembly:

```bash
cargo build --target wasm32-unknown-unknown --release
```

This command generates a `.wasm` binary in the `target/wasm32-unknown-unknown/release/` directory. ### Generating JavaScript Bindings

To allow JavaScript to interact with your Rust code, use the `wasm-bindgen` tool to generate the necessary bindings:

```bash
wasm-bindgen                target/wasm32-unknown-unknown/release/wasm_interop_example.wasm --out-dir pkg -- nodejs
```

This command produces output files necessary for JavaScript interoperability, including a JavaScript file and a TypeScript definition file in the `pkg` directory.

Integrating with JavaScript

Now that we have our Rust function compiled and the JavaScript bindings generated, let's create an HTML file to test it out.

Create an `index.html` file in your project root with the following content:

```html
<!DOCTYPE html>
<html lang="en">
<head>
<meta charset="UTF-8">
<meta name="viewport" content="width=device-width, initial-scale=1.0">
<title>Wasm Interop Example</title>
</head>
<body>
<h1>Wasm Interoperability Example</h1>
<script type="module">
import init, { add } from './pkg/wasm_interop_example.js';
async function run() {
// Initialize the wasm module await init();
// Call the Rust function const result = add(5, 7);
console.log(`The result of 5 + 7 is: ${result}`);
}
run();
```

128

```
</script>
</body>
</html>
```

In this HTML file, we load the generated JavaScript module from the `pkg` directory and call the `add` function, logging the result to the console.

Serving the Application

To view your application, you can use a simple HTTP server. You can install a lightweight server like `http-server`:

```bash
npm install -g http-server
```

Then, run the server in your project directory:

```bash http-server
```

Open your browser and navigate to `http://localhost:8080` (or whichever port is specified). You should see the output in the console.

Advanced Interoperability: Calling JavaScript from Rust

In addition to calling Rust functions from JavaScript, `wasm-bindgen` allows you to call JavaScript functions and manipulate JavaScript objects from Rust.

Example: Using JavaScript Console from Rust

Here's a simple example of how you can log messages to the JavaScript console from Rust:

Update your `lib.rs` file:

```rust
use          wasm_bindgen::prelude::*;          use
wasm_bindgen::JsValue;

#[wasm_bindgen] extern "C" {

#[wasm_bindgen(js_namespace  =  console)]  fn  log(s:
&str);

}

#[wasm_bindgen]

pub fn greet(name: &str) { log(&format!("Hello, {}!",
name));

}
```

Here, we define an external function that binds to the JavaScript console's `log` method. The `greet` function will log a greeting message.

Rebuilding the Project

Compile and generate bindings once again to see your changes:

```bash
cargo build --target wasm32-unknown-unknown --release

wasm-bindgen                    target/wasm32-unknown-
unknown/release/wasm_interop_example.wasm    --out-
dir pkg -- nodejs
```

```
```
Updating the HTML File Update your `index.html`:
```html
<!-- ... existing code ... -->
<script type="module">
import init, { add, greet } from './pkg/wasm_interop_example.js';
async function run() { await init();
console.log(`The result of 5 + 7 is: ${add(5, 7)}`);

greet("World");
}
run();
</script>
<!-- ... existing code ... -->
```
```

Reload your webpage, and now you should see both the addition result and the greeting message in the browser console.

With `wasm-bindgen`, Rust and JavaScript can work harmoniously, allowing you to utilize the performance benefits of Rust within the JavaScript ecosystem. By defining functions in Rust, creating seamless bindings, and leveraging JavaScript features, you can create high-performance web applications that maintain responsiveness and interactivity.
```

In this chapter, we explored the setup process, the syntax for exposing Rust functions to JavaScript, how to call JavaScript functions from Rust, and how to manage data interchangeably between the two languages. As the WebAssembly ecosystem matures, the combination of Rust and JavaScript through `wasm-bindgen` becomes an increasingly compelling technology stack for web developers.

Creating and Using WebAssembly Modules in Modern Web Frameworks

This chapter delves into creating and using WebAssembly modules in modern web frameworks, particularly focusing on Rust—a systems programming language that offers safety and performance characteristics ideal for WebAssembly development.

Understanding WebAssembly

WebAssembly is a binary instruction format designed for stack-based virtual machines. It allows code written in languages like Rust, C, and C++ to run on the web at near-native speed, providing a powerful performance boost compared to JavaScript. WebAssembly modules can be executed directly in web browsers, delivering functionalities previously unattainable due to performance constraints.

Key Features of WebAssembly

Portability: WebAssembly modules are designed to be portable across various platforms that support the WebAssembly runtime.

Security: Designed with a sandbox execution model, WebAssembly runs securely in web browsers.

Performance: Offers near-native performance, making it suitable for compute-intensive applications such as gaming, image processing, and more.

Why Use Rust for WebAssembly?

Rust is gaining popularity for WebAssembly development due to several compelling reasons:

Memory Safety: Rust's ownership model ensures memory safety, preventing common bugs such as null pointer dereferencing and buffer overflows.

Concurrency: Rust's concurrency model allows for safe parallel programming, enabling developers to leverage multi-core processors effectively.

Rich Ecosystem: The Rust ecosystem provides libraries and tools that integrate well with WebAssembly, such as `wasm-bindgen` for JavaScript bindings and `wasm-pack` for packaging Rust code into WebAssembly.

Setting Up the Development Environment

To begin creating WebAssembly modules in Rust, you'll need to set up your development environment. Here are the steps to get started:

Install Rust:

First, install Rust using `rustup`, the Rust toolchain installer. Run the following command in your terminal:

```bash
curl --proto '=https' --tlsv1.2 -sSf https://sh.rustup.rs | sh
```

```

```

Follow the on-screen instructions to complete the installation.

Install WebAssembly target:

Next, add the WebAssembly target by running the following command:

```bash
rustup target add wasm32-unknown-unknown
```

Install `wasm-pack`:

`wasm-pack` simplifies building and packaging Rust-generated WebAssembly. Install it using Cargo:

```bash
cargo install wasm-pack
```

Set Up the Project:

Create a new Rust project using Cargo:

```bash
cargo new rust_wasm_example --lib cd rust_wasm_example
```

Open the `Cargo.toml` file and add the following dependencies:

```toml [dependencies]
wasm-bindgen = "0.2"
```

134

```
```

Creating a Simple WebAssembly Module

Now that your development environment is set up, let's create a simple WebAssembly module that provides basic arithmetic operations.

Write Rust Code:

Open `src/lib.rs` and write the following code:

```rust
use wasm_bindgen::prelude::*;

#[wasm_bindgen]
pub fn add(a: i32, b: i32) -> i32 { a + b
}

#[wasm_bindgen]
pub fn subtract(a: i32, b: i32) -> i32 { a - b
}
```

The `wasm_bindgen` attribute makes the functions accessible from JavaScript.

Build the Project:

Use `wasm-pack` to build the project:

```bash
wasm-pack build --target web
```

This command creates a `pkg` directory containing the

compiled WebAssembly module and JavaScript bindings.

Using WebAssembly in Modern Web Frameworks ### Integrating with a Web Framework

Let's integrate the WebAssembly module with a modern web framework like React. Follow these steps:

Set Up a React App:

Create a new React application using Create React App:

```bash
npx create-react-app rust-wasm-react cd rust-wasm-react
```

Install Dependencies:

Install the necessary packages to load WebAssembly modules:

```bash
npm install @wasm-tool/wasm-pack-plugin
```

Configure Webpack:

Open `webpack.config.js` and add the `wasm-pack-plugin`:

```javascript
const WasmPackPlugin = require('@wasm-tool/wasm-pack-plugin');

module.exports = {
// other config... plugins: [
new WasmPackPlugin({
```

```
    crateDirectory:        path.resolve(_____dirname,
    '../rust_wasm_example'),
  }),
],
};
```
``` ` ` ` ```

Load WebAssembly in React:

Create a new component `Calculator.js` to call the Rust functions:

```javascript
import React, { useState } from 'react';

import init, { add, subtract } from 'rust_wasm_example';

const Calculator = () => {  const [a, setA] = useState(0);
const [b, setB] = useState(0);

const [result, setResult] = useState(null);

const loadWasm = async () => { await init();

};

const calculateAddition = () => { setResult(add(a, b));

};

const calculateSubtraction = () => { setResult(subtract(a,
b));

};

return (
```
```

```javascript
<div>
<h2>Rust WebAssembly Calculator</h2>
<input value={a} onChange={(e) =>
setA(parseInt(e.target.value, 10))} />
<input value={b} onChange={(e) =>
setB(parseInt(e.target.value, 10))} />
<button onClick={calculateAddition}>Add</button>
<button
onClick={calculateSubtraction}>Subtract</button>
<p>Result: {result}</p>
<button onClick={loadWasm}>Load WASM</button>
</div>
);
};
export default Calculator;
```

Render the Component:

Finally, update `App.js` to include the `Calculator` component:

```javascript
import React from 'react';
import Calculator from './Calculator';
function App() { return (
<div className="App">
```

138

```
<Calculator ></Calculator>
</div>
);
}
export default App;
```

Running the Application

To see your application in action, run the following command in your React project directory:

```bash
npm start
```

Visit `http://localhost:3000` in your web browser, where you should see the calculator. Load the WebAssembly module and try adding or subtracting two numbers!

The synergy between Rust and WebAssembly not only enhances application performance but also leverages Rust's safety features. As the ecosystem continues to grow, developers are encouraged to explore these powerful tools that promise to reshape how we build web applications.

Chapter 9: WebAssembly Memory Management and Efficient Usage

In this chapter, we will delve into how memory is managed in Wasm, explore Rust's behavior regarding memory allocation, and learn best practices for maximizing performance in WebAssembly applications.

9.1 Overview of WebAssembly Memory

WebAssembly defines a linear memory model, which can be thought of as a contiguous block of bytes that can be dynamically resized but does not expose the complexities of traditional memory management systems like heap and stack fragmentation. Instead, memory in WebAssembly is managed through a single, linear array of bytes accessible through specific APIs.

9.1.1 Linear Memory

In WebAssembly, linear memory can be thought of as an array of bytes. It is initialized at a minimum size, and its size can be grown using the `grow` instruction. However, it cannot be shrunk. The linear memory model operates under a simple principle: everything is a byte, and the developer is responsible for interpreting that byte array as needed (e.g., integers, floats, or custom data structures). This requires careful planning when allocating memory for various data types.

9.1.2 Importing and Managing Memory

WebAssembly allows developers to import memory from the host environment, which can provide additional flexibility. For instance, a WebAssembly module might use memory allocated by a JavaScript environment that calls into native functions. This can be important for performance optimization, especially when dealing with large datasets or frequent memory operations.

9.2 Memory Management in Rust for WebAssembly

In the Rust programming language, memory safety is a key feature, which is particularly valuable for developers working with WebAssembly where performance and safety are paramount. Rust's ownership model and the borrow checker help prevent data races and other concurrency issues, which translates well into the context of Wasm.

9.2.1 Allocating Memory

When compiling Rust to WebAssembly, developers must keep in mind that the way Rust allocates memory can differ significantly from typical applications. The Rust standard library's memory allocation functions might not be available unless specifically included. Therefore, using the `wee_alloc` crate can significantly reduce the compiled size of the Wasm binary, making it more efficient for web applications.

To allocate memory explicitly in Rust for WebAssembly, developers use the following methods:

Using `alloc` crate: The `alloc` crate, which provides collections and utilities that manage memory efficiently, can be utilized along with the `web-sys` crate to handle WebAssembly memory.

Data Layout: Understanding the data layout in Wasm is crucial. Rust's data structures must be carefully designed to ensure they overlay correctly in the linear memory space.

9.2.2 Deallocating Memory

While Rust's ownership model facilitates automatic deallocation of memory when data goes out of scope, developers targeting Wasm must be careful. WebAssembly itself does not have the same garbage collection mechanisms available in languages like JavaScript or Python. As a result:

Manual Deallocation: Developers need to manually manage the allocation and deallocation of memory to prevent leaks. The Rust standard library provides tools to create and manage user-defined memory pools in Wasm.

Avoiding Fragmentation: When using dynamic memory, be mindful of fragmentation. Strategies such as object pooling can reduce fragmentation and improve performance.

9.2.3 Interfacing with JavaScript

Proper interfacing between Rust and JavaScript through WebAssembly can help manage memory efficiently. When passing data between these two environments, it's essential to minimize copies to avoid unnecessary performance overhead. Using shared memory or transferring ownership of buffers can help mitigate performance hits.

9.3 Strategies for Efficient Memory Usage in Rust WebAssembly

To make the most of memory when developing Rust applications for WebAssembly, there are several strategies to consider.

9.3.1 Optimize Data Structures

Using compact data structures can minimize memory footprint. For instance, choosing smaller primitive types or specialized collections can lead to reduced memory usage. Consider employing:

Fixed-size arrays instead of vectors when the size is known at compile time.

Enumerations to represent multiple states efficiently instead of using larger types. ### 9.3.2 Minimize Allocations

Reducing the frequency and size of memory allocations can have significant performance benefits. Techniques include:

Batch processing items to reduce the overhead of repeated allocations.

Using Stack Allocation where feasible, as stack allocation can be faster and more efficient compared to heap allocation.

9.3.3 Use Memory Pools

For applications with a predictable allocation pattern, implementing memory pools can greatly improve the efficiency of allocation and deallocation. This technique involves creating a fixed-size pool of memory and allocating from it rather than calling the general-purpose allocator.

9.4 Profiling and Debugging Memory Usage

Profiling memory usage is crucial for identifying performance bottlenecks and issues within a WebAssembly application. Rust's integration with tools such as `wasm-bindgen` and `wasm-opt`, along with JavaScript tools for performance analysis, provide developers with valuable insights.

Using Debug Symbols: When compiling for development, including the `--debug` flag can help expose Rust's memory management behavior.

Browser Developer Tools: Utilize browser tools to monitor memory allocation, look for leaks, and gauge performance impacts of various memory operations.

By leveraging Rust's memory safety guarantees and employing strategic memory management techniques, developers can create efficient WebAssembly applications that deliver exceptional performance on the web.

Understanding WebAssembly Linear Memory and Its Operations

In this chapter, we will explore WebAssembly's linear memory, how it is represented and managed in Rust, and the operations you can perform within this memory model.

What is Linear Memory in WebAssembly?

WebAssembly linear memory is a contiguous and mutable block of memory that can be accessed by a Wasm module. Think of linear memory as a one-dimensional array of bytes, which is indexed by an unsigned integer. This model stands in contrast to traditional memory management in high-level languages, where complex structures such as stacks and heaps are often not explicitly controlled by the programmer.

In WebAssembly, linear memory has a few key characteristics:

Contiguous: All memory is laid out in a single continuous array. This simplicity aids in performance and predictability.

Resizable: While it starts at a defined size, linear memory can be resized dynamically to accommodate the needs of the application—subject to certain constraints.

Typed as Bytes: All memory operations deal in bytes, requiring developers to manage the layout and interpretation of data types manually.

Linear Memory in Rust

Rust, a systems programming language designed for safety and concurrency, offers excellent tooling for compiling to WebAssembly. It provides abstractions that make it easier to work with linear memory, while still giving developers low-level control.

Declaring Linear Memory in Rust

When writing a Rust project to be compiled into WebAssembly, you typically use the `wasm-bindgen` crate or the `std::alloc` module for memory management. To define linear memory:

```rust
#![no_std] // Use no standard library extern crate wasmer_runtime;

use core::mem; #[no_mangle]

pub extern "C" fn allocate(size: usize) -> *mut u8 {

let layout = std::alloc::Layout::from_size_align(size,
```

```
mcm::align_of::<u8>()).unwrap();            unsafe         {
std::alloc::alloc(layout) }
}
```
` ` `

Here, we declare an `allocate` function that takes a size argument and allocates a specified number of bytes in linear memory.

Accessing and Manipulating Linear Memory

Once you have linear memory set up, accessing and manipulating data is straightforward. Rust's safety features help ensure that operations are valid, although managing memory requires some diligence.

Read and Write Operations

To read from and write to linear memory, you can use slices to represent sections of memory. For example, suppose you want to store an array of integers in linear memory:

```rust
#[no_mangle]
pub extern "C" fn store_data(ptr: *mut i32, len: usize) {
let slice = unsafe { std::slice::from_raw_parts_mut(ptr, len) }; for i in 0..len {
slice[i] = (i * 2) as i32; // Store double the index value
}
}
#[no_mangle]
pub extern "C" fn fetch_data(ptr: *const i32, len: usize) ->
```

```
i32 { let slice = unsafe { std::slice::from_raw_parts(ptr,
len) }; slice.iter().sum() // Return the sum of the array
}
```

In this example, `store_data` populates linear memory
with double the index values, while `fetch_data` sums up
the values stored at that memory location.

Resizing Linear Memory

The ability to resize linear memory in a WebAssembly
module is another powerful feature, allowing dynamic
allocation based on user needs. Rust makes this relatively
straightforward, though you must ensure you correctly
manage memory to avoid leaks or invalid access:

```rust
#[no_mangle]
pub extern "C" fn resize_memory(new_size: usize) { let
old_size = current_memory();

if new_size > old_size {

resize(new_size); // Hypothetical resize function

}

}
```

Safety Considerations

Memory safety is a core feature of Rust, which extends to
WebAssembly's linear memory. Incorrect memory
handling can lead to buffer overflows or out-of-bounds
access, resulting in undefined behavior. To mitigate these
risks, Rust's borrow checker and ownership model enforce

strict rules, but it is still crucial to be vigilant when dealing with raw pointers and unsafe code blocks.

Native Interoperability

WebAssembly enables different languages to coexist within the same runtime environment. Rust's seamless integration with JavaScript through `wasm-bindgen` allows developers to manage linear memory with techniques familiar to them while leveraging the performance of a compiler-optimized Wasm module:

```rust #[wasm_bindgen]

pub fn js_function_call(arr: &[i32]) -> i32 {
arr.iter().map(|&num| num * 2).sum()

}
```

In this example, a JavaScript function can receive data directly from memory, process it, and return results—allowing for rapid iterations between the two languages.

Understanding linear memory in WebAssembly and its operations in Rust is fundamental for building efficient, low-level applications that run inside web browsers. While Rust provides tools and abstractions, a solid grasp of both memory management and the principles of WebAssembly are essential for creating robust, high-performance software.

Strategies for Managing Memory in High-Performance Applications

This chapter explores various strategies for managing memory in high-performance applications using Rust, ensuring optimal performance while maintaining safety and reliability.

1. Understanding Rust's Ownership Model

Before delving into specific strategies, it's essential to grasp Rust's ownership model, which is at the core of its memory management concept. The ownership model is built upon three primary principles:

Ownership: Each piece of data in Rust has a single owner, a variable responsible for managing its memory.

Borrowing: References to a data owner can be borrowed immutably or mutably, allowing data to be accessed without transferring ownership.

Lifetimes: Rust uses lifetimes to ensure that references do not outlive the data they point to, preventing dangling references and data races.

By understanding these concepts, developers can leverage Rust's compiler checks to write memory-efficient and safe code.

2. Stack vs. Heap Memory

Rust uses two primary regions for memory allocation: the stack and the heap.

Stack Memory: This is where variables with known sizes at compile time are stored. Memory allocation on the stack is fast since it follows a simple Last-In-First-Out (LIFO) order, and memory is automatically reclaimed when variables go out of scope.

Heap Memory: This is used for data whose size may

not be known at compile time. Allocating and deallocating memory on the heap is slower than on the stack, which can lead to performance bottlenecks if not managed properly.

Strategy: Use Stack Memory When Possible

To enhance performance, prioritize the use of stack memory by declaring variables with known, fixed sizes. For instance, using arrays and tuples can leverage stack allocation, reducing the overhead of heap allocations.

```rust
fn main() {

let numbers: [i32; 3] = [1, 2, 3]; // Stack allocation let tuple: (i32, i32) = (10, 20); // Stack allocation

}
```

3. Efficient Use of Heap Memory

When heap memory is necessary, using smart pointers such as `Box`, `Rc`, and `Arc` can help manage memory efficiently:

Box<T>: Use `Box<T>` for heap-allocated single values when ownership is required. This reduces memory overhead and allows for dynamic allocation without manual management.

Rc<T> and Arc<T>: When multiple ownership is necessary, `Rc<T>` (single-threaded) and `Arc<T>` (thread-safe) enable shared ownership without manual reference counting. However, both come with a performance cost due to additional overhead.

Strategy: Minimize Heap Allocations

To reduce the performance penalties associated with heap allocations, consider using the following techniques:

Use Local Buffers: Keep temporary variables or buffers as local stack variables to minimize heap usage.

Preallocate Collections: When using collections like `Vec`, consider preallocating space using methods like `with_capacity()` to avoid repeated allocations during growth.

```rust
fn main() {

let mut numbers = Vec::with_capacity(100);   // Preallocate space for i in 0..100 {

numbers.push(i);

}

}
```

Reuse Memory: Implement object pools or other mechanisms to reuse memory instead of allocating and deallocating frequently.

4. Understanding Rust's Memory Safety Features

Rust's memory safety guarantees via its borrow checker mitigate many common memory issues, such as use-after-free or data races. However, understanding when and how memory is allocated based on ownership can further optimize performance.

Strategy: Analyze Memory Usage with Tools

To track and analyze memory usage, use tools like `cargo valgrind`, `heaptrack`, or `gperftools` to profile your application. Analyzing memory usage reveals patterns that can be adjusted for more efficient management.

```bash
cargo build --release

valgrind --leak-check=full target/release/my_application
```

5. Leveraging Zero-Cost Abstractions

Rust's design aims to provide abstractions (like iterators or combinators) without runtime overhead. Carefully exploiting Rust's zero-cost abstractions enables writing expressive, high-level code while maintaining performance.

Strategy: Use Iterators and Adaptors

Instead of manually iterating with loops, using Rust's iterator patterns can yield performance benefits due to optimizations in the compiler. For example, using `map`, `filter`, and `fold` can lead to more readable and often more optimized code.

```rust
fn square_numbers(numbers: &[i32]) -> Vec<i32> {
numbers.iter().map(|&x| x * x).collect()
}
```

```
```

6. Concurrency and Parallelism

High-performance applications often require concurrent execution. Rust's safety guarantees make it particularly well-suited for multithreading by preventing data races at compile time.

Strategy: Use Threads and Async

Utilizing Rust's `std::thread` for parallel computations can significantly enhance performance. For I/O-bound applications, take advantage of asynchronous programming with the `async` and `await` keywords.

```rust
use std::thread;

fn main() {

let handle = thread::spawn(|| {

// Thread work here...

});


handle.join().unwrap(); // Wait for the thread to complete

}
```

By understanding Rust's ownership model, utilizing stack and heap memory efficiently, leveraging memory safety features, and taking advantage of concurrency, developers can achieve optimal performance while maintaining the safety guarantees that Rust provides. Implementing these strategies in your application will not only improve performance but also lead to more reliable and maintainable code.

Chapter 10: Security Considerations in Rust WebAssembly Applications

This chapter aims to provide an overview of the security model inherent to WebAssembly, the specific considerations for Rust developers, and the best practices for ensuring a robust security posture in your applications.

10.1 Understanding WebAssembly Security Model

WebAssembly is designed with security in mind, creating a sandboxed environment that executes code in a controlled manner. The core of the WebAssembly security model revolves around the following principles:

10.1.1 Sandboxing

WebAssembly runs in a secure sandbox, isolating it from the host environment. This means that Wasm code cannot access the file system, network, or other critical system resources directly. Such isolation helps prevent malicious code from compromising the host system, as it lacks the permissions to perform unauthorized actions.

10.1.2 Memory Safety

Rust is known for its strong emphasis on memory safety, and when compiled to WebAssembly, these guarantees remain intact. Rust's ownership model and borrow checker ensure safe memory access, which helps mitigate common vulnerabilities like buffer overflows or use-after-free errors. However, developers must remain vigilant, as subtle bugs can still lead to safety issues.

10.1.3 Type Safety

WebAssembly enforces strict type checking, which

155

enhances the security of applications. This means that type-related bugs that can be exploited at runtime are less likely to occur, reducing the attack surface. Rust's static typing amplifies this security by allowing developers to catch type-related issues at compile-time.

10.2 Potential Vulnerabilities in WebAssembly

Even with the robust security model of WebAssembly, some vulnerabilities may arise, often due to the interactions between Wasm code and the JavaScript environment. Here are several potential vulnerabilities to keep in mind:

10.2.1 Code Injection

As WebAssembly applications may interact with dynamic data from web sources, developers must ensure that untrusted input data is not improperly handled. This includes validating and sanitizing all inputs to protect against code injection attacks, such as those that could force a Wasm module to execute unintended operations.

10.2.2 Improper Privilege Escalation

While WebAssembly is sandboxed, errors in the JavaScript code that interfaces with WebAssembly can inadvertently expose privileged operations or data. It is crucial to implement proper access control and validation at the JavaScript boundary to mitigate the risk of privilege escalation attacks.

10.2.3 Denial of Service (DoS)

WebAssembly's ability to execute complex logic can lead to potential denial of service vulnerabilities, where attackers can exploit the application's logic to consume excessive resources. Implementing timeouts and limits on resource utilization within Wasm can help protect against such attacks.

10.3 Rust-Specific Security Best Practices

Given Rust's unique features and the nature of WebAssembly applications, developers should consider the following best practices to bolster security:

10.3.1 Use the Latest Stable Rust Version

Always compile your Wasm applications with the latest stable version of Rust, as this ensures you benefit from the latest performance improvements, security patches, and bug fixes.

10.3.2 Avoid Using Unsafe Code

Rust provides the ability to write "unsafe" code, which bypasses the compiler's safety checks. While necessary for certain low-level tasks, using unsafe code increases the risk of vulnerabilities. Limit its use to cases where it is absolutely necessary, and document thoroughly why it is needed.

10.3.3 Minimize Dependencies

Each dependency you add to your Rust project introduces potential vulnerabilities. Regularly audit your dependencies with tools such as `cargo audit`, and remove any that are unnecessary or lack community maintenance.

10.3.4 Conduct Thorough Testing

Implement a comprehensive testing strategy that includes unit tests, integration tests, and end-to-end tests. Use fuzz testing to expose potential vulnerabilities that might not be evident through traditional testing methods.

10.3.5 Secure Compilation

Use secure compilation settings, such as enabling optimizations (-O2 or -O3), which can help minimize the size and complexity of generated Wasm binaries. Consider using tools like `wasm-opt` to optimize the Wasm output further, reducing the attack surface of the produced binary.

10.3.6 Leverage WebAssembly Security Features

Utilize the built-in security features of WebAssembly, such as the `--no-signature` option when compiling binaries that do not require external library interactions, and leverage memory management tools provided by Rust's ecosystem.

While WebAssembly offers a secure execution environment, the responsibility falls on developers to maintain good security hygiene through best practices and rigorous testing. By understanding the potential vulnerabilities and employing effective strategies, Rust developers can harness the power of WebAssembly while safeguarding their applications from malicious threats.

Best Practices for Secure WebAssembly Development

This chapter discusses best practices for secure WebAssembly development in Rust, aiming to ensure that applications not only perform well but are also resilient to potential attacks.

Understanding WebAssembly and Rust

Before diving into best practices, it's essential to understand the architecture of WebAssembly and how Rust fits into the picture. WebAssembly is designed to run in a safe, sandboxed environment. This makes it resistant to classic vulnerabilities such as buffer overflows. Rust enhances these features with its ownership model, which prevents data races and ensures memory safety.

While Rust's safety guarantees are robust, developers must still be vigilant in their approach to security, as vulnerabilities can arise from poorly written code, external libraries, or the integration of WebAssembly with other web technologies.

1. Leverage Rust's Ownership and Borrowing System

Rust's ownership model is one of its most significant advantages when it comes to security. This model enforces strict rules at compile time regarding how memory is accessed and managed, which helps prevent common vulnerabilities such as buffer overflows and use-after-free errors.

Best Practices:

Use ownership patterns: Ensure that all data is properly owned, borrowed, or transferred. Avoid using `unsafe` blocks unless absolutely necessary, as they bypass Rust's safety checks.

Limit mutable references: Use immutable references wherever possible, as this reduces the risk of unintended side effects and concurrent access issues.

Prefer slices and safer abstractions: Use Rust's slice types instead of raw pointers to minimize risks associated with direct memory access.

2. Follow the Principle of Least Privilege

When developing WebAssembly applications, it is crucial to adhere to the principle of least privilege. This principle dictates that a piece of code should have only the necessary permissions to perform its tasks.

Best Practices:

Use sandboxes: Run your WebAssembly modules in a securely configured sandbox to limit their access to potentially sensitive operations.

Limit exports and imports: Only export the functions that are necessary and minimize the number of imports required in your WebAssembly modules.

Control memory access: Be judicious with memory usage and ensure that your Wasm module does not inadvertently expose sensitive data through shared memory.

3. Validate and Sanitize Inputs

Any external data, especially input from users, can be a potential attack vector. This risk remains even in a secure language like Rust, especially when operating in the dynamic web environment.

Best Practices:

Validate inputs rigorously: Create strict type and range checks for all incoming data. Use libraries like

`regex` for pattern matching and sanitization.

Handle errors gracefully: Rust's `Result` and `Option` types can help manage errors without panicking. Use error handling to prevent crashes and unintended behavior.

Avoid user-controlled memory allocation: If possible, avoid allowing users to allocate memory or control significant structures to mitigate risks of denial-of-service attacks or other exploits.

4. Use Safe Libraries and Frameworks

Rust's ecosystem includes a wealth of libraries and frameworks designed with security in mind. Utilizing these can help ensure you're adhering to best security practices without reinventing the wheel.

Best Practices:

Choose libraries wisely: Use libraries that follow sound security practices and are well-maintained. Check for known vulnerabilities using tools like `cargo audit`.

Prefer stable APIs: When integrating third-party libraries, prefer those that use stable APIs and have a good reputation for security.

Regularly update dependencies: Keep dependencies up to date to ensure that you benefit from security patches and improvements.

5. Audit and Test Your Code

Regular audits and testing are essential components of any secure development process. In addition to relying on Rust's type safety, proactive testing and code examination can identify potential issues before they become actual vulnerabilities.

Best Practices:

Perform static analysis: Use static analysis tools to detect coding errors, vulnerabilities, and compliance issues before deployment.

Conduct code reviews: Regularly review code with a focus on security. Peer reviews can often reveal potential security issues overlooked by the original author.

Implement fuzz testing: Use fuzz testing tools to generate unexpected inputs and stress test your application's response.

Consider formal verification: For critical components, consider using formal verification methods to mathematically prove the correctness and security of the code.

6. Monitor and Update Deployed Applications

Security is not a one-time effort; it requires continuous monitoring and updates. After deployment, it's vital to stay vigilant for new vulnerabilities or security advisories related to your dependencies.

Best Practices:

Monitor application behavior: Implement logging and monitoring to catch anomalies in application behavior that may indicate a security breach.

Stay informed about vulnerabilities: Subscribe to

security feeds and mailing lists relevant to Rust and WebAssembly to be aware of the latest advisories.

Plan for incident response: Prepare a strategy for responding to potential incidents. Ensure that you can quickly patch vulnerabilities and inform users as needed.

By adhering to the best practices outlined in this chapter—leveraging Rust's unique safety features, following the principle of least privilege, validating inputs, choosing safe libraries, conducting audits and tests, and monitoring deployed applications—developers can significantly mitigate risks and create secure, efficient applications that harness the full power of WebAssembly.

Mitigating Vulnerabilities and Exploits in WebAssembly Applications

Rust, with its emphasis on safety, concurrency, and performance, has naturally aligned itself with WebAssembly development. However, the intersection of WebAssembly and Rust also brings forth unique challenges and potential vulnerabilities that developers must be aware of.

In this chapter, we will explore best practices and strategies for mitigating vulnerabilities and exploits in WebAssembly applications written in Rust. We will start by defining common threats and weaknesses that can arise in this environment, followed by a detailed examination of mitigation strategies, tooling, and techniques that developers can employ to secure their applications.

5.1 Understanding Potential Vulnerabilities ### 5.1.1 Memory Safety Issues

While Rust is designed to eliminate many common memory safety issues, when compiling to WebAssembly, developers may still inadvertently introduce vulnerabilities related to memory misuse. This includes buffer overflows, use-after-free errors, and uninitialized memory access. Such vulnerabilities can lead to arbitrary code execution in malicious contexts.

5.1.2 Logic Flaws

Logic flaws can also affect WebAssembly applications. Rust developers must ensure that their logic prevents unauthorized access to critical paths in their code, maintains data integrity, and adheres to proper authentication and authorization standards.

5.1.3 Man-in-the-Middle (MitM) Attacks

Though WebAssembly itself runs in a safe execution environment, applications may still be susceptible to network-based attacks. If data exchanged between the client and server is not properly encrypted, it may be intercepted and manipulated by malicious actors.

5.1.4 Dependency Vulnerabilities

Rust projects often rely on external crates from the Cargo package manager. While the Rust ecosystem is robust, vulnerabilities in dependencies can lead to serious security flaws in your application. Keeping track of known vulnerabilities in dependencies is crucial.

5.2 Mitigation Strategies

5.2.1 Comprehensive Testing and Auditing

A thorough testing process is essential for any application, particularly those written in Rust and compiled to

WebAssembly. Employ the following practices:

Unit Testing: Ensure that each module is tested independently to catch potential logic flaws early.

Integration Testing: Test how modules interact to identify issues that may not be apparent when modules are tested in isolation.

Fuzz Testing: Use fuzz testing tools like American Fuzzy Lop (AFL) or Cargo-fuzz to identify unexpected behaviors and edge cases.

5.2.2 Employing Rust's Safety Features

Take full advantage of Rust's memory safety features by adhering to its ownership model, appropriately using lifetimes, and relying on the borrow checker. This will help prevent many memory-related vulnerabilities. Use constructs like `Option` and `Result` to handle errors gracefully instead of bypassing error handling.

5.2.3 Use of WASM Sandboxing

WebAssembly runs in a secure sandboxed environment, but additional security can be achieved by utilizing libraries and runtimes that enhance this sandboxing. Tools like Wasmtime or Wasmer allow for fine-grained control over the execution environment, including resource limits and access controls.

5.2.4 Implement Secure Data Handling Practices

Data Encryption: Always encrypt sensitive data both in transit and at rest. Utilize secure protocols such as HTTPS and WebSockets over TLS.

Input Validation: Rigorously validate all inputs to prevent injection attacks and ensure that data adheres to expected formats before processing.

Output Encoding: Encode outputs to prevent Cross-Site Scripting (XSS) vulnerabilities. ### 5.2.5 Dependency Management

Regularly audit your dependencies using tools like `cargo-audit` to identify vulnerabilities in third-party crates. Set up Dependabot or similar tools for automated notifications about vulnerabilities in dependencies.

5.3 Utilizing Tooling for Enhanced Security ### 5.3.1 Built-in Rust Tools

Rust offers built-in tools for identifying and mitigating vulnerabilities:

Clippy: A linter that helps catch common mistakes and enforces best practices.

Rustfmt: A tool for formatting Rust code that can help alleviate some readability issues that might hide vulnerabilities.

5.3.2 Static and Dynamic Analysis Tools

Integrate static analysis tools like `cargo clippy` and `cargo audit` into your development process. For dynamic analysis, consider tools like `wasm-opt` to optimize WebAssembly module size, which can sometimes uncover inefficiencies or oversights in the code.

5.3.3 CORS Policies

Configure Cross-Origin Resource Sharing (CORS) policies carefully to control the resources accessible from other origins. Implement strict policies that limit the origins allowed to fetch your WebAssembly modules and APIs.

5.3.4 Continuous Integration and Continuous Deployment (CI/CD)

Adopt CI/CD practices to automate builds and tests, ensuring that any vulnerabilities can be detected and addressed promptly. Automated testing can also help track regressions that may introduce new vulnerabilities.

While this partnership offers high performance and safety, developers must remain vigilant against potential vulnerabilities and exploits. By adopting secure coding practices, leveraging Rust's robust tooling, conducting thorough testing, and maintaining strong dependency management, developers can create resilient WebAssembly applications capable of withstanding a range of threats.

Conclusion

As we reach the end of this journey through "Rust Programming for Web Assembly: Build Blazing-Fast, Next-Gen Web Applications," we hope you have gained valuable insights into the powerful capabilities that Rust and WebAssembly bring to the world of web development. We have explored how Rust's performance, safety, and concurrency features make it an ideal choice for building modern web applications, while WebAssembly allows developers to run high-performance code in the browser.

Throughout this ebook, we have walked through essential concepts, from setting up your development environment to writing efficient code that leverages the strengths of both Rust and WebAssembly. You have learned how to create responsive, high-performance applications capable of handling complex computations and delivering unparalleled user experiences.

The landscape of web technology is evolving rapidly, and the combination of Rust and WebAssembly is at the forefront of this transformation. As you continue your journey in building applications with these technologies, remember that the web is not just about rendering content—it's about creating engaging, interactive experiences that push the boundaries of what's possible.

We encourage you to experiment with the projects we covered, explore additional libraries, and contribute to the vibrant Rust and WebAssembly communities. The knowledge and skills you have gained from this ebook are just the beginning. Embrace the challenges ahead, stay curious, and keep pushing the envelope in your web development endeavors.

Thank you for joining us on this exploration of Rust and WebAssembly. We wish you success in your journey to create blazing-fast, next-generation web applications that inspire and captivate users across the globe. Happy coding!

Biography

Jeff Stuart is a visionary writer and seasoned web developer with a passion for crafting dynamic and user-centric web applications. With years of hands-on experience in the tech industry, Jeff has mastered the art of problem-solving through code, specializing in Rust programming and cutting-edge web technologies. His expertise lies in creating efficient, scalable, and secure solutions that push the boundaries of what web applications can achieve.

As a lifelong learner and tech enthusiast, Jeff thrives on exploring the ever-evolving landscape of programming languages and frameworks. When he's not immersed in writing code or brainstorming innovative ideas, you'll find him sharing his knowledge through inspiring content that empowers others to unlock their full potential in the digital world.

Beyond his professional pursuits, Jeff enjoys exploring the art of minimalist design, reading thought-provoking books on technology and philosophy, and hiking to recharge his creative energies. His unwavering dedication to excellence and his belief in the transformative power of technology shine through in every page of his work, making this book a compelling guide for anyone eager to master the art of Rust programming and web development.

Glossary: Rust Programming for Web Assembly

A

AssemblyScript: A TypeScript-like language that compiles to WebAssembly. It provides an alternative for developers familiar with TypeScript to build applications for the WebAssembly ecosystem.

Asynchronous: Refers to operations that are non-blocking, allowing the program to continue executing while waiting for a response or resource. Rust's async features enable developers to build efficient and responsive applications.

B

Bloat: The increase in application size due to unnecessary code or library dependencies. In a WebAssembly context, keeping an application light and free of bloat is crucial for performance.

Binary format: WebAssembly is a binary instruction format for a stack-based virtual machine. It is designed to be a portable compilation target for high-level languages like Rust.

C

Cargo: The package manager and build system for Rust. Cargo is essential for managing dependencies, building projects, and packaging Rust applications for WebAssembly.

Crate: A package or library in Rust. Crates can be created for various purposes, including those tailored for WebAssembly development.

D

Debugger: A tool that allows developers to inspect code execution, set breakpoints, and evaluate expressions to resolve issues in applications. Debugging WASM can present unique challenges due to its binary nature.

DOM (Document Object Model): A programming interface for web documents. It represents the structure of a document and allows languages like JavaScript to manipulate HTML and XML documents.

E

Emscripten: A toolchain that compiles C/C++ code to WebAssembly, enabling the use of existing libraries and applications written in those languages alongside Rust.

F

Function Signature: The definition of a function that specifies its name, parameters, and return type. Understanding function signatures is crucial when importing or exporting functions between Rust and JavaScript.

Framebuffer: A portion of memory used for storing image data that will be displayed on the screen. In a WebAssembly context, it may be used in graphics rendering.

G

Garbage Collection (GC): An automatic memory management feature. Rust does not use garbage collection but employs ownership, borrowing, and lifetimes concepts to manage memory safely.

H

Heap: A region of memory used for dynamic memory allocation. Rust's ownership model makes heap management safe and efficient, even when programming for WebAssembly.

I

Imports and Exports: WebAssembly modules can import functions or variables from the host environment, such as JavaScript. Conversely, they can export functions or variables for the host environment to use.

J

JavaScript (JS)**: A high-level programming language widely used for web development. It often interacts with WebAssembly modules, serving as a bridge between the web page and low-level WebAssembly code.

L

LLVM (Low-Level Virtual Machine)**: A compiler infrastructure used by Rust to compile its code into WebAssembly. Rust's compilation to LLVM allows for optimizations and interoperability with various platforms.

M

Memory**: In the context of WebAssembly, memory is a linear array of bytes used for storing data. Rust's memory model ensures that developers can work with WebAssembly's memory safely.

Module**: A standalone unit in WebAssembly that contains functions and data. Modules are the primary way that code is organized for execution in the WebAssembly runtime.

O

Ownership**: A core concept in Rust that ensures memory safety without needing a garbage collector. Ownership is crucial when dealing with memory in WebAssembly, helping to prevent memory leaks and data races.

P

Performance**: An essential aspect of any application, especially in web development. Rust's performance characteristics make it a suitable choice for building WebAssembly applications.

Panic: A situation in Rust where the program encounters an unrecoverable error. Understanding how to handle panics is important when developing resilient applications in WebAssembly.

R

Rendering: The process of generating visual output from a given source, such as HTML or graphics. WebAssembly can enhance rendering performance for graphics-intensive applications.

Runtime: The environment in which a program executes. The WebAssembly runtime allows for executing WASM binaries in various contexts, including browsers and servers.

S

Stack: A region of memory used for storing temporary data such as function parameters, local variables, and return addresses. Rust manages the stack carefully to ensure memory safety.

WebAssembly System Interface (WASI): A set of system calls for WebAssembly modules that enables them to perform tasks like file management, network operations, and more in a secure and portable manner.

T

Toolchain: A set of tools used for building and managing projects. In Rust, the toolchain includes the Rust compiler (rustc), Cargo, and various libraries needed for developing WebAssembly applications.

V

Vector: A dynamically sized array in Rust. Working

with vectors can be essential in WebAssembly, especially for applications that require flexible data structures.

W

WebAssembly: A binary instruction format designed to be a portable compilation target for high-level languages. It enables high-performance execution in web browsers and other environments.

www.ingramcontent.com/pod-product-compliance
Lightning Source LLC
La Vergne TN
LVHW022346060326
832902LV00022B/4270